The Rule of Paw Bible
[7 in 1]

The Dog Training Rulebook with Mental and Physical Exercises, Including All about Dog Nutrition and a Delicious Cookbook.

Table of Contents

Introduction

Are you a dog owner who's tired of dealing with a furry little tornado wreaking havoc in your home? Do you feel like you're constantly picking up chewed-up shoes, cleaning up messes, and dealing with disobedient behavior? Are you struggling with potty training? Are you at your wit's end with your dog's bad behavior? Are you worried about feeding your dog a healthy and nutritious diet? Look no further.

These bad days with your pup can be a thing of the past. This book makes this alternate reality possible for you.

Welcome to THE COMPLETE DOG BIBLE - the ultimate guide with seven books wrapped up in one neat package. The following pages include training, mental and physical exercises, nutrition, cooking, and so much more for your furry best friend! Say goodbye to chewed-up shoes, endless cleaning, and disobedient behavior, and say hello to a happy, healthy, and well-trained dog...and by extension, a happy dog mom or dad – you. This book is a one-stop-shop for everything you need to know about raising a happy, healthy, and well-behaved pup.

For easy reading and references, the book has been sectioned into 7 parts:
1. From Breed to Bedtime: A Guide to Choosing the Right Dog and Preparing Your Home
2. Training Through the Ages: Building Trust from Neonatal to Adult
3. Reading Between the Woofs: Understanding Dog Body Language and Behavior
4. Toys and Treats: Finding the Right Playthings for Your Pup
5. Let the Games Begin! A Guide to Fun and Interactive Games for Your Dog
6. From Bowls to Bellies: A Guide to Nourishing Your Pup
7. Fido's Feast: Gourmet, Nutritious, and Delicious Recipes for Your Canine Companion

As dog owners, we all want the same thing - for our dogs to be well-behaved and healthy. But let's face it, sometimes training your dog can feel like an uphill battle. From potty training to leash manners, it can be overwhelming to know where to begin. That's where this book comes in. I've gathered the most effective training methods from expert trainers to help you teach your dog everything from basic obedience to advanced tricks.

But training is just the beginning. To have a well-rounded, healthy pup, you need to focus on their physical and mental health as well. That's why I've included a section on physical exercises that will keep your dog in tip-top shape and provide an outlet for their boundless energy. From agility training to swimming, I've got exercises that will keep your dog engaged, happy, and healthy.

But mental exercises are just as important as physical ones. Dogs are intelligent creatures who need to be intellectually stimulated to be happy and well-behaved. That's why a section on mental exercises is included. Following the outlined strategies will challenge your dog's mind and engage him or her. From scent games to puzzle toys, I've got exercises to help your dog stay mentally sharp and happy.

Of course, none of this is possible without proper nutrition. A balanced diet is the foundation of your dog's health, and I've got you covered. I've included a diet section covering everything from choosing the right food to preparing meals for your dog at home.

And finally, what's a book on dog training and health without a cookbook section? I've included a cookbook section with recipes that are delicious and nutritious for your furry friend. From basic meals to gourmet treats, I've got something for every occasion.

So, THE COMPLETE DOG BIBLE has something for you. I believe every dog deserves to live their best life, and I'm here to help you make that happen.

Let's start this journey of helping your pup live his or her best life together! Turn the page.

Part 🐾

from Breed to Bedtime:
A Guide to Choosing the Right Dog and
Preparing Your Home

Seasoned pooch proprietor? Fresh-faced pup caregiver? It does not matter which one you are because one thing is for sure - choosing the right breed and preparing your home can be ruff. (Sorry, I couldn't resist a good pun.) But don't worry. With a little guidance and a lot of love, you'll be on your way to creating the ultimate home for your furry best friend. This part of the book was designed specifically for that purpose.

So, grab a chew toy, kick back, and get ready to learn everything you need to know from breed to bedtime. Trust me, your future canine companion will thank you (with lots of tail wags and sloppy kisses).

Choosing The Right Breed

Are you ready to add a furry friend to your family but feel overwhelmed by all the different breeds out there? Don't worry; I've got you covered! In this chapter, I'll guide you through the process of choosing the right breed for your lifestyle and personality.

Whether you're a couch potato or an avid adventurer, a pup out, there is perfect for you. I'll help you narrow your options based on activity level, size, grooming needs, and temperament.

No matter which of the breeds you choose, one thing's for sure: they're sure to bring endless love and laughter into your life. So, let's dive in and find the furry friend that will make your heart skip a beat!

Why Does Choosing the Right Breed Matter?

Choosing the right dog breed is a decision that can have a major impact on your life. It's not something you should take lightly, like choosing what flavor of ice cream to have for dessert. No, no, no, this is much more serious. But don't worry; I'm here to guide you through the process and explain the importance of choosing the right breed.

First, we can talk about why this decision is so crucial. You see, different breeds of dogs have different personalities and characteristics that are inherent to their breed. For example, a Beagle and a Bullmastiff will have very different needs and temperaments. If you're not prepared to meet those needs and deal with their natures, things could get hairy pretty quickly.

So, before you start searching for your fur-ever friend, consider these factors.

1. <u>Lifestyle</u> – Are you a homebody or prefer to embark on exciting adventures often? Do you have a big backyard or live in a small apartment? These are all essential things to consider when choosing a breed to love. Some breeds require lots of exercise and stimulation, while others are content lounging around all day.

2. <u>Size</u> - Do you want a lap dog or a dog that could double as a small horse? The size of your dog will impact everything from how much space they need to how much food they eat. Plus, small dogs may be more fragile and require extra care and attention.

3. <u>Energy level</u> - Do you want a dog that's always on the go or one that's more laid-back? If you're an active person who wants a companion for hiking and running, a high-energy breed like a Border Collie or a Dalmatian might be a good fit. But if you're looking for a dog to snuggle up with on the couch, a breed like a Bulldog or a Basset Hound might be more your speed.

4. <u>Temperament</u> - Different breeds have different temperaments that may or may not be suited to your lifestyle. Some breeds are naturally more friendly and extroverted, while others are more reserved or aggressive. It's essential to do your research and opt for a breed that matches your personality and energy level.

5. <u>Grooming needs</u> - Would you mind brushing and grooming your dog, or would you instead they were low-maintenance? Some breeds require daily grooming to keep their coat healthy and shiny, while others are content with a quick brush now and then.

I will expand on these factors and more in upcoming sections.

Once you've considered all these factors, you can start your search for the perfect breed. And remember, just because a breed is trendy doesn't mean it's the right fit for you. Do your research and talk to other dog owners to get an idea of what living with that breed is really like.

You might think, "But what if I fall in love with a breed that doesn't match my lifestyle?" That's where compromise and creativity come in. For example, if you live in a small apartment but love a breed that needs lots of space to run, consider finding a nearby dog park or hiring a dog walker to help meet their exercise needs. Or, if you have allergies but love a breed with a lot of fur, look into hypoallergenic breeds or invest in a good air purifier.

At the end of the day, choosing the right breed is all about setting yourself and your new furry friend up for success. You want to create a happy and healthy home for them, and that starts with choosing a breed that matches your way of life and disposition.

So, think hard, do your research, and make the best decision. Your perfect pup is out there waiting for you, and with a little effort and patience, you and that pup will make that love match.

Size Matters

Size does matter when it comes to picking the right dog for you and your lifestyle.

How about we start by discussing the petite pups? These tiny puppies are cute, cuddly, and oh-so-portable. They're great for apartment living and for those who want a lap dog to snuggle up on the couch. However, don't let their small size fool you - they can still pack a punch in terms of energy and personality. Small breeds like Chihuahuas and Yorkies are known for their feisty attitudes and spunky personalities. On the other hand, their tiny size means they don't require as much food, which can be a plus for those on a budget.

Moving on, it's time to discuss medium-sized breeds. These dogs are the perfect size- not too big and not too small, they are perfect! Medium breeds like Beagles and Border Collies are great for families with kids and those who want a dog that's not too small but not too large. They're also great for those who want an active and energetic dog but not so much that they need a huge yard to run around in. Medium breeds can be great companions for those who love to go on walks or hikes, and they're also great for those who want a smart and easy dog to train.

Finally, we have large breeds. These majestic pups are the kings and queens of the dog world. Great Danes and St. Bernards are just a few examples of large breeds, and they're great for those who have lots of space and lots of love to give. Large breeds are also great for those who want a protective and loyal dog, as they can make great guard dogs. However, their size also means that they require lots of food and lots of exercise, so they're not ideal for those who live in small apartments or don't have much free time to spend with their furry friend.

So, when it comes to size, it's important to consider your living situation, your lifestyle, and your preferences. Think about how much space you have, how much time you can devote to your dog, and what kind of personality you want in a pet. With a little bit of study and much love, you're sure to find the perfect dog for you!

Temperament and Personality

You want to find a dog that fits your lifestyle and personality well, right? So, temperament and personality are two important factors that you should definitely take into consideration when it comes to choosing the right dog breed for you.

First up for discussion are active breeds. These dogs have a lot of energy and require plenty of exercise and stimulation to stay happy and healthy. If you're an active person who loves spending time outdoors and going on long hikes, then an active breed might be a good choice for you. Breeds like the Jack Russell Terrier, Australian Shepherd, and Border Collie are known for their high energy levels and love for playtime.

But if you're more bound to your home or prefer to spend your days binge-watching your favorite TV shows, then a laid-back breed might be more your style. These dogs tend to be more mellow and content with relaxing at home. Breeds like the Basset Hound, Bulldog, and Great Dane have monopolized the territory for easygoing personalities and a love for lounging around.

On the other hand, if you like their space and independence, then an independent breed might be a better fit for you. These dogs tend to be more self-sufficient and less needy than other breeds. Breeds like the Shiba Inu, Afghan Hound, and Chow Chow would fit such a personality well.

But if you're a social butterfly who loves being around people and other animals, a social breed might be more your speed. These dogs are outgoing and love being around their human companions and other dogs. Breeds like the Beagle, Pug, and Havalese fit in this grouping.

A note of caution is necessary to end this section. Every dog is different from any other and may not correspond to a specific breed stereotype. It's always a good idea to meet a dog and spend time with them before deciding, regardless of their breed or personality.

Grooming Needs

Let's talk about something that's really important when choosing the right breed for you: grooming needs. It's not just about having a cute and cuddly dog. You have to make sure you're responsible for keeping that furball clean and groomed.

Let's start by discussing breeds with short hair. These pups may seem low-maintenance, but don't let their short coats fool you. They still need regular brushing to maintain a shiny and healthy coat. Plus, short-haired breeds tend to shed a lot, so if you don't want your home to be covered in dog hair, you'll need to keep up with the vacuuming.

Onto the long-haired breeds. These dogs can be quite a handful when it comes to grooming. They need frequent brushing to prevent matting and tangling and may also require regular haircuts. And let's not forget about the hair that will inevitably end up all over your clothes and furniture. If you're up for the challenge of keeping up with the grooming needs of a long-haired breed, then go for it. But if you're unwilling to put in the time and effort, it might be best to choose a shorter-haired breed.

There are also breeds with special grooming requirements. These dogs require extra attention when keeping them clean and tidy. Take the poodle, for example. These dogs need regular haircuts and grooming to keep their curly coats looking their best. And then there's the Chinese Crested, which may not have much hair but still needs regular bathing and skin care to keep their sensitive skin healthy.

Grooming is not only beneficial for your dog's beauty but also for its health. Regular grooming can help prevent skin infections and other health issues. So, it's important to consider a breed's grooming needs before bringing them home.

Health and Lifespan

Health and lifespan are the ultimate factor combo to consider when choosing a dog breed. After all, you don't want to get too attached to a furry friend who will only be around for a few years or one who will end up costing you a fortune in vet bills.

Before we delve into anything else, let's take a closer look at some common health concerns. Every breed has different health apprehensions. Some breeds are prone to hip dysplasia (a genetic condition where a dog's hip joint doesn't fit together properly, causing pain and difficulty in movement), others to respiratory issues, and some to allergies. But don't worry; there are ways to stack the deck in your favor.

One option is to go with a mixed breed. A mixed breed has the best of the two words. You get a unique look and a mix of genes that can reduce the likelihood of health problems. It's like getting a genetic cocktail but without the hangover.

Next, let's talk about lifespan. This is tricky because no matter what breed you choose, it's never long enough. But it's important to plan accordingly to know the average lifespan of different breeds.

For example, a Great Dane may steal your heart with their big, soulful eyes and gentle demeanor, but they typically only live 6-8 years. On the other hand, a small breed like a Chihuahua can live up to 20 years. That's a big difference!

But here's the thing, just because a breed has a shorter lifespan doesn't mean they're not worth considering. They can still be amazing companions and bring much joy to your life.
So, when it comes to choosing the right breed based on health and lifespan, it's all about finding the right balance. You want to choose a breed that fits your lifestyle and personality but also one that has a good chance of being healthy and living a long, happy life.

Living Arrangements

First, let's dive into dog breeds that are a good fit for compact living quarters. If you're living in an apartment or a small home, you'll want a breed that doesn't need a lot of room to roam. Enter the pint-sized pups! Small breeds like Chihuahuas, Pomeranians, and Yorkshire Terriers are great choices for those with limited living space. They are cute and cuddly and don't require much exercise, making them perfect for a cozy apartment.

But what if you have a bigger home or outdoor space? Fear not; there are plenty of breeds that will thrive in a larger living area. If you've got a yard, you might want to consider a breed that loves to run and play, like a Labrador Retriever or a Border Collie. These energetic breeds need plenty of exercise and stimulation, so if you've got the space and time to give them what they need, they'll be your loyal life companion.

Now, let's discuss some breeds that can adapt to either living arrangement. Those live happily both in an apartment and in a big house. The French Bulldog, for example, is a small breed that doesn't require a lot of space but doesn't need much exercise. They're perfectly content snuggling up on the couch with you or going for a stroll around the block.

On the flip side, there are larger breeds that can adapt to living in a smaller space if they get enough exercise and attention. The Greyhound, for example, is a breed that loves to run but is also known for being couch potatoes. They don't need a lot of room to run around in as long as they get plenty of exercise in other ways.

So, when it comes to living arrangements, choosing a breed that fits your specific lifestyle is important. Consider the size of your living space, the amount of exercise you're able to provide, and the personality of the breed you're interested in. With so many different breeds to choose from, you're sure to find one that's the perfect fit for you and your living situation.

And remember, no matter what breed you choose, they will love you unconditionally - even if you're living in a shoebox!

Compatibility with Children and Other Pets

When it comes to adding a furry friend to your family, it's important to consider how they'll get along with other members of your household. Will your new pup be a good match for your kids or other pets? Let's explore the world of dog breeds and see which ones are compatible with children and other pets.

Let's start by discussing breeds famous for their childhood-friendly personalities. If you have little ones running around, you want a dog that will be gentle and patient with them. Some breeds that fit the bill include the Irish Setters, Beagle, and Golden Retriever. These breeds are known for their sweet and affectionate personalities, making them great companions for kids. Plus, they're often very playful and energetic, so they'll have no problem keeping up with your little ones.

But what if you already have pets at home? Will your new dog get along with them? The answer is... it depends. Some breeds are more social and friendly with other animals, while others prefer to be the only pet in the household. For example, if you have a cat, you might want to consider a breed like the Bichon Frise or the Shih Tzu, both known for their calm and easy-going personalities. If you have another dog, you'll want to look for a breed known for being social and friendly with other canines. Breeds like the Boxer, Bulldog, and Pug are all known for their playful and sociable personalities.

Of course, it's not just about the breed. Every dog has a unique personality, so spending time with your potential new pet is important before deciding. Take them for a walk, play with them, and see how they react to your kids or other pets. Bring your kids or other pets along to meet the dog before you bring them home if you can. This can help you get a sense of how they'll all get along.

When it comes to kids and pets, it's important to remember that both need to be appropriately trained. Explain to your kids how to behave with dogs securely and lovingly. This means no pulling tails or ears, roughhousing, or approaching strange dogs without permission. Similarly, ensure your new dog is trained to behave appropriately around kids and other pets. This means teaching them basic commands like "sit" and "stay" and socializing them with other animals and people from a young age.

Training and Exercise Needs

Training and exercise are things that make every dog owner's life a little more interesting. Some breeds just seem to get it right away, while others need a little more coaxing to behave. And don't even get me started on exercise needs. Some pups are content with a stroll around the block, while others need a full-blown marathon to tire them out.

If you're a new dog owner, you might prefer a breed that is easy to train. After all, not many of us have the time and energy to spend trying to teach our furry friend to sit, stay, and rollover. Don't worry! Many breeds learn on their own. They pick up on commands quickly and love to please their humans. Think of them as the A+ students of the dog world. Some breeds are highly intelligent and trainable.

But then there are those breeds that need a little more work. You know, the ones that make you wonder if they're just pretending not to understand. I'm looking at you, Basset Hound. These dogs are known for being obstinate and autonomous, making training a bit of a challenge. But with patience and consistency, even the most headstrong pup can learn to follow commands. And honestly, the sense of accomplishment you'll feel when your Basset finally masters "stay" is worth all the effort.

Now, let's talk about exercise needs. Some breeds are content with a short walk around in the garden, while others need a full-blown workout to be happy. If you're a couch potato who's looking for a dog that will binge-watch Netflix with you, you might want to steer clear of breeds like the Border Collie or Australian Shepherd. These pups were bred to work and needed a ton of stimulation to be happy.

But what if you're an active person who's looking for a running buddy? Well, then, you might want to consider breeds like the Dalmatian or Weimaraner. These dogs were bred to run and have loads of energy to burn. Just be prepared for them to leave you in the dust as they sprint ahead.

Of course, there are plenty of breeds that fall somewhere in between these two extremes. Breeds like the Labrador Retriever and Boxer are known for their energy and athleticism, but they're also happy to curl up on the couch with their humans when the workout is done.

A Few More Thoughts

We've covered a lot of ground in this part of the book already. From the importance of choosing the right breed, to size, temperament, grooming, health, living arrangements, and training needs, we've left no tail unturned. But before we wrap up this chapter, I have a few final thoughts to share with you.

First off, I want to encourage you to consider adoption from your local animal shelter or rescue organization. Not only will you be giving a loving home to a deserving pup, but you'll also be doing your part to help reduce the number of dogs in shelters. Plus, you never know what kind of furry friend you'll find waiting for you at the shelter.

I also want to remind you of the value of responsible breeding practices. Puppy mills and irresponsible breeders contribute to overpopulation, often resulting in unhealthy dogs with behavioral issues. So, if you decide to purchase a purebred dog, be sure to find a creditable breeder who prefers the pups' well-being and health.

And finally, I want to emphasize the importance of choosing the best breed for you and your needs. As tempting as it is to choose a breed based solely on looks or popularity, it's important to remember each breed's unique personality, energy level, and grooming needs. Considering these factors sets you and your furry friend up for a happy and healthy life together. After all, whether you're a couch potato, marathon runner, city dweller, or country bumpkin, there's a breed out there that's perfect for you. You just need to research, choose responsibly, and most importantly, have fun finding the little (or not so little) guy (or girl)! After all, what's life without a little slobbery love and wagging tails?

So now that you've got a pretty good idea of what breed might be right for you, it's time to start thinking about where you're going to get your new furry friend from. Let's discuss that in the next chapter.

Kennel Or Breeding?

Picture this: you're in the market for a new puppy and torn between going to a breeder or a kennel. But wait, what's the difference between the two? Don't they both just sell adorable little balls of fluff? Well, yes and no.

A kennel is a place where multiple dogs are kept in individual cages or runs. Think of it like a hotel for dogs. Some kennels are just boarding facilities where you can leave your pup briefly while you're out of town. But some kennels breed dogs for sale.

On the other hand, a breeder is someone who focuses on producing purebred dogs with specific traits and characteristics. They usually have a smaller number of dogs that are kept as part of their family, and they often have a waiting list for their puppies.

Now, let's talk about why making the right choice is important when deciding where to get your new furry friend. When you adopt a puppy, you're committing to take care of them forever. You want to ensure that you're getting a healthy puppy from a reputable source, which means doing your research.

So, what should you consider when deciding between a kennel or a breeder? Well, here are a few things to keep in mind:

1. <u>Health</u>: You want to ensure your new puppy is healthy and free of genetic or hereditary diseases. Reputable breeders will have their dogs' health tested and will be able to provide you with documentation. On the other hand, Kennels may not be as thorough with their health checks.

2. <u>Socialization</u>: Puppies need to be socialized from a young age to ensure that they grow up to be well-adjusted adults. Breeders typically have a more hands-on approach to socialization, as their puppies are raised in their homes with their families. Kennels may not have the same level of socialization opportunities.

3. <u>Cost</u>: Let's be real; puppies aren't cheap. You'll want to consider the cost of purchasing a puppy from a breeder versus a kennel. While breeders may charge more upfront, you may save money in the long run if your puppy is healthy and well-socialized.

4. <u>Ethics</u>: It's important to consider the ethics of where you're getting your puppy from. Reputable breeders will prefer the pups' well-being and health, while some kennels may focus more on profit.

So, whether you go with a breeder or a kennel, do your research and choose a source that prioritizes the health and happiness of their dogs. Check out reviews and ratings from other fur-parents. Don't just rely on the website of the kennel or breeder because they're going to try to put their best paw forward. You should know the parents dogs' health history. Ethical breeders will be more than happy to share this information with you. They'll also want to know about your lifestyle and what you're looking for in a new fur baby. This is because they want to ensure their puppies go to good homes where they'll be loved and well-cared for.

And if you're ever in doubt, just remember: if it feels wrong, it probably is. Trust your instincts while doing your research, and you'll end up with a happy and healthy pup who will bring you years of joy and companionship.

This chapter helps you with the research part of things. We'll discuss all you need to consider making the right decision for you. And who knows, maybe you'll end up finding the perfect pet for you and your family!

Kennels

Let's get one thing straight: a kennel is not a place where you adopt a new furry friend and play with cute puppies all day. It's not like a petting zoo. A kennel is basically a fancy word for a facility where dogs are bred and raised for sale. Think of it like a puppy factory, but hopefully with a little more love and care involved.

Don't get me wrong; there are some pros to getting a puppy from a kennel. For one, they often offer health guarantees, which means that if your pup gets sick within a certain timeframe, they'll take care of it. Plus, they usually have a variety of breeds to choose from, so you can find the perfect match for your lifestyle and needs.

But, as with anything in life, there are also some cons to consider. The biggest issue with kennels is the potential for puppy mills. These are dog breeding operations prioritizing money over the dogs' well-being. It's a sad reality, but some kennels are just in it for the money and don't care about the health or happiness of their animals.

Another potential downside is the lack of socialization. Puppies raised in kennels may not have had much interaction with humans or other dogs, which can lead to behavioral issues later on. It's important to ensure that the kennel you choose provides plenty of socialization opportunities for their puppies.

So, what should you consider when choosing a kennel? First and foremost, reputation is key. Make sure that the kennel you're considering has a good track record and is known for producing healthy, happy puppies. Cleanliness is also important - if the kennel looks dirty or unkempt, it's probably not a good sign. And lastly, make sure you get to interface with the puppies before deciding. This will give you a good idea of their temperament and personality, and you'll see firsthand how they've been treated and socialized.

Breeders

It's time to talk about breeders. When I say breeder, I'm talking about someone who purposefully mates dogs to produce puppies. These folks tend to be passionate about their dogs and want to ensure their pups go to loving, responsible homes. However, like any other aspect of life, there are advantages and disadvantages to consider.

Let's start with the pros. One of the biggest benefits of getting a puppy from a breeder is that you'll have a good idea of the parents' health history. Good breeders will do genetic testing to ensure their dogs are healthy and free of potential genetic issues. They'll also ensure that the puppies receive proper socialization so they're well-adjusted and ready to take on the world.

Another benefit of going with a breeder is that you'll have more options when it comes to choosing a breed. Breeders tend to specialize in specific breeds, so if you have your heart set on a certain type of pup, chances are you'll be able to find a breeder who specializes in that breed.

There are downsides to consider, too. One of the biggest concerns with breeders is the potential for unethical breeding practices. Money may be placed over their dogs' well-being and health. Some breeders may cut corners regarding genetic testing or may breed dogs who are not healthy or well-suited for breeding.

Another downside of going with a breeder is that they can be more expensive than going with a kennel. You may pay more to buy a breeder's puppy because breeders are more specialized. Additionally, there may be a longer wait time to get a puppy from a breeder, especially if they have a popular breed.

So, how do you choose a breeder? Like with kennels, reputation is central. Look for good breeders who are transparent about their breeding practices. You must know the parent dogs' health history and ensure they've been genetically tested. And, of course, ensure that the breeder is a good fit for you and your family.

So, you've done your research and decided where to get your new furry friend. Now, it's time to prepare your home for their arrival. In the next chapter, I'll go over some essential tips and tricks for home preparation.

Home Preparation

Congratulations! You've decided to welcome a furry friend into your home. Don't worry if you feel disoriented. I'm here to help. Let's start with the basics: home preparation.

First up, the kitchen. This is where you'll be preparing your pup's meals, so it's important to make sure it's a safe and accessible space for them. Keep toxic foods (like chocolate and onions) out of reach, and invest in sturdy bowls that won't tip over easily. It's also a good idea to designate a specific spot for your pup's food and water so they know where to go during mealtime.

Let's move on to the living space. This is where you and your pup will spend a lot of time together. Make it cozy and comfortable. Invest in durable, washable furniture, like couch covers and throw pillows, to protect your belongings from accidents or shedding. And don't forget to provide plenty of toys and comfortable bedding for your furry friend to snuggle up with.

The bathroom is one of the most important areas to prepare, as it's where your pup will be doing their business. Get high-quality cleaning supplies and designate a specific spot outside for your pup to go potty. If you live in an apartment or don't have easy access to a yard, consider investing in some pee pads or a grass patch to make things easier.

Moving on to the bedroom. This is where you and your pup will be sleeping. This needs to be a secure and pleasant space for both of you. Look into getting sturdy and washable bedding and ensure any loose cords or wires are out of reach. If you plan on crate training your pup, get a comfortable and appropriately sized crate for them to sleep in.

Last but not least is the wardrobe. Yes, you read that right. Your pup will need its own wardrobe! Get your new puppy comfortable and durable collars and leashes, and consider getting a harness if your pup is a puller. Remember to buy nail clippers, brushes, shampoo, and other grooming supplies. Your pup might not love getting groomed, but it's a necessary evil for them to remain healthy and happy.

Now that we've covered the basics let's talk about some extra steps you can take to prepare your home for your furry friend. First and foremost, ensure you're up to date on any necessary vaccinations and have a plan for regular vet checkups. It's also an excellent idea to puppy-proof your home by covering exposed wires, securing cabinets and drawers, and ensuring any plants are safe for dogs.

And finally, consider investing in some training classes or working with a professional trainer to help your pup adjust to their new home and learn some basic obedience skills. Remember, bringing a new pup into your home is a big responsibility. Still, with some preparation and lots of love, it can be a gratifying experience for you and your furry friend.

You've got your home all set up and ready for your pup, but now what? Well, just like humans, dogs go through different stages of development as they age, and each stage comes with its own set of challenges and opportunities. So, in the next chapter, we'll dive into the world of dog training through different ages, from puppyhood to seniorhood.

Part 2

Training Through the Ages:
Building Trust from Neonatal to Adult

Unfortunately, as much as we'd like to believe our adorable little puppies will stay that way forever, they do grow up. And just like human children, our furry friends go through different phases of development, from the neonatal stage to the rebellious teenage years (yes, even dogs have them) and all the way to adulthood.

But fear not, because with some patience, perseverance, and maybe a treat or two, you can train your pup through any age and build a lifelong bond. This part of the book was written to help you get through all these stages and phases like the dog training pro you were destined to be.

Training Fundamentals

Whether you've just brought home a brand-new puppy or are dealing with an adult dog who still hasn't quite figured out how to behave, training is key to a happy and healthy relationship between you and your furry friend.

But training isn't a one-size-fits-all approach. The techniques that work for a rambunctious puppy may not be the same for an adult dog with a bit more life experience. That's why it's important to understand the different stages of a dog's life and tailor your training methods accordingly.

In this chapter, we'll dive into the neonatal, puppy, teenage, and adult stages of a dog's life, discussing the unique challenges and opportunities that come with each. This chapter will provide the knowledge and tools you need to train your dog through every stage of its life. So, grab a treat (or two or three), and let's start!

Neonatal Stage (0-2 weeks)

The neonatal stage is like the newborn phase of humans but with more fur and fewer diapers. During this stage, puppies are between 0 and 2 weeks old and about as helpless as a squirrel trying to cross a busy street. They can't see or hear very well yet and rely on their mom for everything.

As a responsible pet parent, giving these little guys the best possible start in life is essential. That means providing a warm and safe environment, ensuring they get enough milk (or formula if they're not with their mom), and handling them gently to help with early socialization.

Socialization is key during this stage. Puppies exposed to different sights, sounds, and smells during this time are more likely to be well-adjusted and confident as they grow older. So go ahead, and introduce them to the vacuum cleaner, the TV, and maybe even the blender. Just be sure to do it in a calm and controlled way.

Oh, and when it comes to feeding, be prepared for some round-the-clock bottle or nursing sessions. These little ones must eat every few hours, just like human babies. But don't worry; seeing those cute little puppy bellies full and happy is worth it.

Puppy Stage (3-12 weeks)

The puppy stage is a time of adorable yips and wiggly tails. But don't let those cute little faces fool you - this is a critical time in your pup's life. From 3 to 12 weeks, your puppy develops necessary social and behavioral skills that will stick with them for life.

That's right. Socialization is key during this stage as well. Expose your pup to as many people, places, and things as possible to help them become confident and well-adjusted adult dog. And don't forget basic obedience training! It may seem silly to teach a tiny ball of fluff to sit or come when called, but it's worth it in the long run.

Now, let's talk about housebreaking. Ah, the joys of cleaning up puppy messes. But fear not. With consistent training and positive reinforcement, you can teach your pup to do its business outside (or on a designated pee pad, if that's your thing). And crate training can be a lifesaver for both you and your pup. It provides a safe and secure place to rest and can help with housebreaking by teaching them to hold their bladder.
So, embrace the chaos of the puppy stage and get to training! Your pup will be forever grateful.

Teenage Stage (3-6 months)

The teenage stage. We've all been there, right? Pimples, awkward growth spurts, and the urge to rebel against authority. Well, guess what? Dogs go through that phase too! During the teenage stage, your pup is trying to assert its independence and test its boundaries. They might try to chew up your favorite shoes or jump on the couch, but it's all a part of their development.

As responsible owners, it's important to continue their socialization during this time. Take them to new places, introduce them to new people and animals, and help them build self-confidence.

It's also time to ramp up their obedience training. Basic commands like "sit" and "stay" should already be second nature, so now it's time to teach them more advanced commands like "heel" and "leave it."

And let's not forget about addressing those pesky problem behaviors. Chewing, jumping, and barking might be cute when tiny, but it's not so adorable when they're bigger. So, start correcting these behaviors before they become ingrained habits.

Adult Dog Stage (6+ months)

The adult stage is a time for independence, maturity, and maybe even some self-discovery. But when it comes to your furry friend, it's also a time for continued learning and training. Just because your dog has grown up doesn't mean they don't need guidance and reinforcement. In fact, the adult stage is when you can see the results of all your hard work paying off (or not paying off, if you slacked on training earlier).

During this stage, it's important to keep up with the good habits you've already established, such as positive reinforcement, consistency, and patience. But you can also take it to the next level with some advanced obedience training, like agility or tricks.

Additionally, you may need to address more complex behavior issues, such as aggression or anxiety, that may have developed over time. Don't be afraid to seek out professional help if needed. Remember, it's never too late to start training and reinforcing good behavior in your adult dog.

As your furry friend continues to grow and learn, it's important to remember that building a strong bond of trust is key to a successful and happy relationship. In the next chapter, we'll explore ways to deepen your connection with your dog and strengthen your bond for years to come.

Creating Trust

As a human, you might communicate through words and facial expressions, but for our furry friends, body language is key. From the way they wag their tails to the position of their ears, dogs are constantly sending signals about how they're feeling. And if we want to build trust with them, we must understand what they're saying. This means getting down and dirty to understand dog behavior and communication. We need to comprehend common fears and anxieties that dogs experience and how to help them through them. Reading your dog's body language puts you in the position to tell when they're happy, scared, or even sick.

So, are you ready to know more about your dog? This chapter will dive into the wonderful world of building trust with your furry friend. You see, trust is the foundation of any healthy relationship, and the same goes for the bond you share with your dog. When your pup trusts you, they'll be more eager to follow your lead, obey your commands, and feel more secure in your presence. Plus, a dog that trusts you is generally happier and more relaxed.

This chapter will explore strategies to help you build trust with your dog, from communication to bonding activities. So, get ready to take notes and start building that special bond with your four-legged companion!

Building Trust through Training

So, you've got yourself a furry companion and want to build a strong bond with them. The key to this is building trust with your dog, which you can do by training. But not just any training. I'm talking about positive reinforcement training.

Positive reinforcement training means that if you reward that behavior, dogs will likely repeat it. Dogs are no exception! And let's be honest, who doesn't love a good reward?

This type of training involves rewarding your dog for doing something right rather than punishing them for doing something wrong. Think of it as a win-win situation. You get a well-behaved dog, and they get lots of treats and praise.

But what kind of training exercises should you be doing to build trust? First, start with the basics. Teach your dog commands like "sit," "stay," and "come" using positive reinforcement. This sets the foundation for more advanced training exercises later on.

Next, focus on exercises that require your dog to come to you, like recall training. This is especially important for building trust because it shows your dog that coming to you is always good.

Another great exercise is tough training. This involves teaching your dog to touch its nose to your hand or a target object and rewarding him. This helps build trust because it prepares your dog to trust you to provide them with positive experiences.

Building Trust through Play

Playing with your dog isn't just a fun way to pass the time – it's also a great way to strengthen your bond and build trust. By engaging in games and activities together, you're providing your dog with much-needed exercise and mental stimulation and creating positive associations between the two of you.

So, what kind of games and activities can you do with your dog to build trust? Here are a few ideas:

1. <u>Hide and Seek</u>: This classic game is a great way to make your dog believe and have confidence in you. While your dog sits, you hide in your garden or house. Then, call his name and wait until he finds you. When they do, recompense them with lots of compliments and a treat.

2. <u>Fetch</u>: You could easily bond with your dog by playing fetch. At first, throw a toy a short distance and stimulate your dog to bring it back to you. Then, when your dog becomes more convinced, you augment the distance and make the game harder.

3. <u>Tug-of-War:</u> While some trainers discourage tug-of-war games when played correctly, it can be a great way to build trust and confidence in your dog. Establish rules (for example, only tug when you say it's okay, stop if your dog's teeth touch your skin, etc.) and use a sturdy toy that won't break easily.

4. <u>Training Games</u>: Incorporating training exercises into your playtime is a great way to reinforce good behavior and build trust. For example, you can practice recall by calling your dog to come to you during a game of fetch or have your dog touch a target with their nose before getting a treat.

Pay attention to their body language when playing with your dog and adjust your play style accordingly. For example, if your dog seems nervous or overwhelmed, take a break and try a different game or activity. And always ensure to end on a constructive note with plenty of compliments and treats.

Building Trust through Bonding Activities

Do you want to take your relationship with your dog to the next level, but you're unsure how? That's where bonding activities come in! Bonding activities are all about spending quality time with your dog and showing them that you're there for them no matter what. These activities can be as simple as giving your dog a good belly rub or as involved as a full-on grooming session. Whatever you choose, the goal is to create a sense of intimacy and closeness between you and your pup.

Grooming is a great bonding activity because it's something that dogs naturally enjoy. You can start by brushing your dog's coat and then move on to cleaning their ears, trimming their nails, and even bathing them. Not only will your dog look and smell better, but they'll also feel more relaxed and comfortable around you.

Another great bonding activity is massage. Just like humans, dogs can benefit from a good rubdown. Massaging your dog can help reduce stress levels, relieve muscle tension, and improve overall health. You can start by massaging your dog's shoulders and back and then move on to its legs and paws. Just be sure to use gentle, soothing strokes, and pay attention to your dog's body language to ensure they enjoy themselves.

Cuddling is another excellent way to build trust with your dog. Dogs crave physical contact, and cuddling is a great way to show your pup that you're there for them. You can cuddle up with your dog on the couch while watching TV or snuggle with them in bed before you sleep. It is important to make sure your dog feels safe and secure and that they know you love them.

Building Trust through Consistency and Reliability

Dogs everywhere can all relate to that feeling of anticipation when their owners promise to take them out for a walk, only to get distracted and leave them waiting with bated breath. While it's common, it is not a healthy situation. Reliability and consistency with our pups are essential to build trust and a strong bond.

Sticking to a consistent routine is one of the best ways to build trust with your dog. This means feeding your pup at the same time every day, taking them for walks regularly, and sticking to a routine your dog can rely on. Consistency helps create a sense of stability and predictability that dogs thrive on, helping them to feel secure and confident.

It's also important to be a reliable and trustworthy owner. Dogs look to us for guidance and leadership, and when we consistently follow through on our commitments, our dogs learn to trust us. This means being on time for feeding and walks, responding to your dog's needs, and consistently showing up for them when they need you.

Another way to build trust through consistency is to establish clear boundaries and rules. When your dog understands what is expected of them, they feel more secure and confident in their place within your household. Consistent rules and boundaries help to create a sense of structure and predictability, which can help reduce anxiety and stress for your pup.

Being a reliable owner also means your dog can trust you to be there when they need you. This means responding to their needs for food, water, or just a little extra attention. It also means being consistent in your interactions with your dog, using positive reinforcement consistently, and avoiding punishment or negative reinforcement.

By now, you and your furry friend should be best buds. You may have even taught them a few neat tricks, like how to fetch your favorite pair of slippers or bark on cue when your least favorite neighbor comes over. But one aspect of your relationship that might cause some tension is potty time. That's right; I'm talking about the "number one" and "number two" situations. So, if you're tired of cleaning up messes around the house or taking your pup on a walk every 20 minutes, it's time to buckle up and get ready for the chapter on potty training. That's up next!

Potty Training

Are you tired of stepping in puddles and piles of your dog's messes? Well, you're not alone! Potty training your furry friend is one of the most important steps in creating a healthy and happy relationship with your dog.

In this chapter, we'll go over the ins and outs of potty training, including tips and tricks to make the process as easy and stress-free as possible. From understanding your dog's needs to creating a consistent routine, we'll cover everything you need to know to help your pup become a potty pro in no time. Grab your poop bags, and let's get started!

Understanding Your Dog's Needs

We all know that a dog's gotta do what a dog's gotta do, but it's up to us to teach them where and when to do it. Every dog is different, but most follow a general bathroom routine. They'll sniff around, circle a few times, and then squat. Keep an eye out for these behaviors so you can quickly lead them to the designated potty spot.

But what if your pup is having accidents inside? It's common for puppies to struggle with potty training, and even adult dogs can have slip-ups. Stay patient and observe their behavior. Maybe they need to go out more frequently or need more positive reinforcement for going outside. It would be best if you also learned to recognize their signals. Some dogs may whine or pace when they need to go out, while others may scratch at the door. Make a note of these signals so you can quickly respond and avoid accidents.

Now that you better understand your dog's bathroom habits and signals, let's move on to the strategies for successful potty training.

Setting Up a Potty-Training Routine

Potty training is a necessary evil of dog ownership. It's a process that requires patience, persistence, and a whole lot of paper towels. But fear not; with a solid routine and some positive reinforcement, you can successfully teach your dog to do its business in the appropriate place.

First, it's important to establish a potty-training routine that works for you and your dog. Dogs thrive on routine, so having a consistent schedule for potty breaks will help them understand when it's time to go. Whether it's every few hours or after meals and naps, find a plan that works for your dog's age and needs.

Crate training can help you with potty training. Dogs naturally avoid going to the bathroom where they sleep, so using a crate can help teach them to hold it until it's time for a designated potty break. Plus, it can keep them out of trouble while you're away from home. But remember, never use the crate as punishment. It should be a safe and comfortable space for your dog, not a place they associate with negative experiences.

Also, establish a designated potty area. This could be a specific spot in your yard or a particular section of your apartment complex. Always bring your dog to the same spot, and he will associate that space with going to the bathroom.

And, of course, positive reinforcement is vital. When your dog successfully goes potty in the designated area, offer praise, treats, or an excellent ol' belly rub. He will learn that going potty in the correct place is right.

Remember that potty training takes a lot of patience and time. Accidents will happen, but staying consistent and positive throughout the process is important. With a little effort and paper towels, your dog will soon be potty trained and ready to take on the world.

Positive Reinforcement Techniques

Nobody wants a house smelling like a dog toilet. Luckily, positive reinforcement can make the process much less painful - for you and your pup. Let's kick off that discussion with reward-based training. If you use positive reinforcement, you'll encourage his good behavior. Think of it like getting an A+ for doing an excellent test at school. Dogs are similar in that they respond well to rewards. So, when your furry friend does their business outside, give them a treat, praise, or a toy as a reward. This helps them link going potty outside with good stuff and drives them to keep doing it.

Another technique for potty training is teaching your dog to go on command. This might sound strange, but it can be helpful, especially if you live in an area with inclement weather. The idea is to teach your dog a specific word or phrase to associate with going potty, so you can use it to prompt him to go when needed. For example, you could use the phrase "do your business" or "go potty" - just be sure to pick something you're comfortable saying in public!

To teach your dog to go on command, start by using the phrase consistently every time they go potty outside. Eventually, they'll start to associate the phrase with the act of going potty. Then, you can start using the phrase to prompt them to go, especially if you're in a rush or the weather is less than ideal.

Remember to be patient with your pup during the potty-training process. They're learning a new skill. That means accidents are bound to happen. When they do, just clean them up with an enzymatic cleaner and move on. Yelling or punishing your dog for accidents will only confuse and scare them, making the potty-training process even harder.

Common Potty-Training Challenges and Solutions

You may have thought you were done with diapers when your kids grew up, but your furry friend has brought them back into your life. Don't worry; I've got some tips to help you through this stinky process.

Accidents are inevitable. Your pup will have a few mishaps along the way. Maybe they get too excited and forget their manners, or perhaps they're just not quite there yet in terms of holding it. Either way, don't get too upset with them. They're still learning and need your patience and guidance.

One solution to accidents is to use a crate. Some people don't like crating their dog but hear me out. A crate can offer dogs a secure and pleasant space because they are den animals by nature. It can also help with potty training by limiting their access to the rest of the house and encouraging them to hold it until you take them outside. Just ensure the crate is the perfect size for your dog, and you don't leave them in there too long.

Another challenge you may encounter is marking. This is when your dog pees on things to claim them as their own. It's more common in male dogs, but females can do it too. So, ensure your dog gets a lot of exercise and mental stimulation. A tired dog is less likely to feel the need to mark their territory. You can also use positive reinforcement to teach them where they should go potty.

Finally, don't give up if you're having trouble with potty training! It's a process and can take some time. Ensure you're consistent with your routine and training techniques, and don't be afraid to ask for help if needed.

With these tips in mind, you and your dog will soon be able to bid farewell to those pesky potty pads and enjoy the freedom of a fully-trained pup.

We've successfully tackled the messy business of potty training your furry friend. Now it's time to focus on the fun stuff - positive reinforcement! Let's dive into the next chapter and discover how to use positive reinforcement to strengthen the bond with your furry friend and encourage good behavior.

Positive Reinforcement

Are you ready to learn about the wonderful world of positive reinforcement for dog training? Of course, you are! Who doesn't love teaching their furry best friend new tricks and behaviors without harsh punishments or negative reinforcement? Positive reinforcement is the best way to train a dog!

In this chapter, we'll explore why positive reinforcement is an effective way to train your dog, how it can benefit you and your furry companion, and some essential strategies for making the most of this approach. Positive reinforcement can build a stronger, more positive relationship with our dogs and turn even the most stubborn pup into a well-behaved and happy family member.

So, let's start on this tail-wagging journey towards effective and positive dog training, where treats and praise are the names of the game. Are you ready? Let's go!

Understanding Positive Reinforcement

Positive reinforcement is one of the most influential and extraordinary techniques for dog training. The idea is that if your furry friend does something good, they'll get rewarded for it. Nothing gets a dog's tail wagging faster than the promise of treats and belly rubs.

But positive reinforcement isn't just about rewarding your pup with treats. It's backed by science! You see when your dog does something good and is rewarded, their brain releases a dopamine hormone. This makes them feel happy and satisfied, making it more likely for them to repeat that good behavior in the future.

So, how do you use positive reinforcement in dog training? Well, the possibilities are endless! From simple commands like sit and stay to more complex tricks like roll over and play dead, positive reinforcement can teach your dog about anything. Some examples of positive reinforcement in dog training include giving your dog treats, praise, and even a good old-fashioned belly rub.

Another crucial aspect of positive reinforcement you must understand is ignoring your dog's bad behavior and redirecting their attention toward good behavior. For example, if your dog is jumping up on people, instead of scolding them, try ignoring the bad behavior and rewarding them when they have all four paws on the ground.

It's important to note that not all rewards will work for every dog. Some dogs may not be food-motivated and may prefer toys or playtime as a reward. Experiment with different reward types and determine what works best for your furry friend.

Timing is also key when it comes to positive reinforcement. The reward must come after every good behavior so your dog can associate behavior and reward. If you wait too long, your dog may not understand why he is being rewarded, and the training may be less effective.

Don't be stingy with the rewards, either. Positive reinforcement is about encouraging good behavior, so ensure your dog knows they're doing something right. Of course, you don't want to overdo it and end up with an overweight dog, but a few extra treats here and there won't hurt.

Teaching New Behaviors

Teaching new behaviors is where the real fun begins! Whether you want to teach your pup how to shake, roll over, or play dead, positive reinforcement is the way to go. The first step to teaching a new behavior is to break it down into smaller, manageable steps. For example, if you teach your dog to lay down on command, then he will easily learn to roll over. Once they've got that down, you can move on to teaching them to roll onto their side. And then, finally, to roll all the way over. By breaking the behavior down into smaller steps, you can make it easier for your dog to understand and learn.

Next, choose the right rewards for your pup. While treats are popular, praise and physical affection can be just as effective. Some dogs might prefer a good scratch behind the ears over a treat any day!

And then there's clicker training. Suppose you've never heard of it. In clicker training, a portable device makes a clicking sound; it's a kind of positive reinforcement training. The click marks the exact moment when your dog does something good and is immediately followed by a reward. The idea is that the click signals your dog that they've done something right, making it easier for them to understand what behavior you're trying to reinforce.

Positive Reinforcement for Problem Behaviors

Oh boy, problem behaviors. Every dog has them, and every owner wishes they didn't. But the good news is that many of these annoying behaviors can be addressed with positive reinforcement.

One typical problem behavior is jumping up on people. It's a natural behavior for dogs but can be frustrating and dangerous when they jump on guests. With positive reinforcement, you can teach your dog an alternative behavior, like sitting politely instead. When your dog greets you with all four paws on the ground, reward him with compliments and treats. Soon enough, they'll learn that sitting politely is the way to get attention and rewards.

Another problem behavior is excessive barking. It's great to have a dog that will alert you to danger, but nobody wants a dog that barks at every little thing. You can train your dog to be quiet on command with positive reinforcement. When your dog starts barking, say "quiet" and wait for them to stop. When they do, give them a treat and praise them. With consistent training, your dog will learn that being quiet is rewarded, and they'll be less likely to bark excessively.

Positive reinforcement can also address destructive behaviors, like chewing on furniture or shoes. Instead of punishing your dog for chewing, give them something they can chew on, like a toy or bone. When they chew on the appropriate object, reward them with treats and praise. This way, they'll learn what's acceptable to chew on and what's not.

Maintaining Positive Reinforcement

You've successfully trained your dog with positive reinforcement, and now they're the best boy or girl ever! But, just like with anything else in life, it's essential to maintain that hard-earned success. You can't just sit back and relax because if you do, your dog might start to forget all the tricks and behaviors you taught them.

So, how do you maintain positive reinforcement training? The answer is consistency. It would help if you continued to use positive reinforcement techniques regularly to reinforce your dog's good behavior. This means giving them treats, praise, and belly rubs every time they do something you want them to do.

Another way to maintain positive reinforcement training is to continue challenging your dog with new behaviors and tricks. Keep their minds active and engaged by teaching them new things, and reward them when they succeed. Remember to break down these new behaviors into smaller, more manageable steps to make learning easier for your dog.

Maintaining positive reinforcement training isn't always easy. There may be times when your dog regresses or forgets a behavior or times when you fail to reward them for doing something good. But don't fret because there are ways to overcome these challenges.

Forgetting to reward your dog for good behavior is common, but it's an easy fix. Try to set reminders on your phone or leave sticky notes around the house as a reminder to give your dog a treat or praise when they do something good. It's also a good idea to keep treats in convenient places, like in your pocket or a treat pouch, so you always have them on hand.

Another challenge is dealing with regression in your dog's behavior. This can happen for various reasons, such as environmental or routine changes. When this happens, go back to the basics and start practicing the behavior again with positive reinforcement. Your dog will eventually remember the behavior and get back on track.

We've covered the importance of positive reinforcement in training our furry friends, but let's not forget the importance of teaching them the key commands they need to succeed. From sit to stay to come, these are the building blocks of effective communication with your pup. Let's get to work on these and more in the next chapter!

Key Commands

Do you know those magical words that turn your furry friend into an obedient, well-behaved pooch? Those are key commands. Key commands are essential for ensuring that your dog understands what you want them to do, whether sitting politely, coming when called, or staying put while you grab their favorite toy.

But here's the thing: training your dog to follow key commands isn't just about impressing your friends and family with your furry friend's skills (although that is a nice bonus). It's also about ensuring the well-being and safety of your dog. When your dog understands and follows key commands, they're less likely to run into dangerous situations, such as running out into traffic or getting into something it shouldn't.

So, what key commands are we going to cover in this chapter? Well, we'll be talking about some of the most fundamental commands, such as sit, stay, come, and heel. These commands are the foundation of any good dog training program and will help you establish a strong bond with your furry friend.

So, grab your pup and get ready to learn some new tricks!

Sit

One of the most basic yet essential commands in a dog's training repertoire is "sit." You might think, "My dog already knows how to sit!" But do they really? I mean, can they sit on command, even when they're distracted by a squirrel or the neighbor's cat? If not, don't worry; I've got you covered.

First, let's talk about why "sit" is an important command. For starters, it's a great way to keep your dog under control in public places. Imagine you're walking down the street, and a stranger approach you. If your dog is trained to sit on command, you can quickly get them to calm down and focus on you instead of the stranger. Additionally, "sit" is a foundational command that can be used as a starting point for other behaviors, like "stay" and "heel."

So, how do we teach our furry friends to sit on command? It's pretty simple. At first, hold a treat near your dog's nose, then move your hand up, down, and back toward their tail. The butt of the dog should lower to the ground while following the treat with its nose. At that precise moment, say "sit" and give him the treat. Repeat many times until your dog sits on command without the treat.

When your dog is sitting on command, it's essential to reinforce the behavior. Every time your dog sits on command, give him lots of praise and a treat. Step-by-step, you can phase out the treats and replace them with praise and love.

But what happens when your dog doesn't want to sit? Well, don't give up! There are a few strategies you can try. First, make sure you're in a quiet, distraction-free environment. You don't want your dog to be distracted by other people or animals. Second, use a cheese or meat treat to motivate your dog. Finally, make sure you're using a firm, clear voice when giving the command. Dogs respond better to a confident tone.

Stay

The "stay" command helps keep your dog out of danger. For example, if you're crossing a busy street or there are other dogs nearby that your pup is itching to play with, you can use the "stay" command to keep them safe and under control.
To teach your furry friend to stay, start by having your dog sit in front of you. Then hold your hand up with your palm facing your dog and give the command "stay." Step back and offer your dog a treat and praise if he stays in place.

If your dog starts to move, say "no" and bring them back to the original spot. You can also use a leash to guide them if they wander gently. Remember to keep the training sessions short and fun for your dog. You don't want to overwhelm them or make them bored.
Once your dog stays in place for a moment, progressively increment the time before rewarding them. You can also try adding distractions, like having someone walk past your dog while they stay. This will help your dog learn to stay focused and ignore distractions.

Reinforce the behavior consistently. Always give your dog a treat and praise when he stays in place, and never reward them if they break the "stay" command. With practice, your dog will start to understand that staying in place is good and will earn them a reward.

Come

The "come" command is a dog owner's dream and a dog's worst nightmare. Why? Well, because there are so many exciting things to sniff and explore that sometimes coming when called just doesn't seem like a priority to our furry friends. But with some positive reinforcement training, you can teach your dog to come when called and look forward to it.

The "come" command is crucial to your dog's safety. So, your dog will stay off the road, in traffic, or in other dangerous situations. Plus, it's just plain convenient. Imagine calling your dog over to you when it's time to leave the park instead of chasing them around for ten minutes.

The key to training your dog to come when called is to make it a positive experience for them. Call their name and praise them when they come to you. As they get the hang of it, gradually increase the distance between you and your dog, and reward them every time they come when called.

It's also important to use a consistent command, such as "come" or "here." Don't use multiple commands for the same action, or your dog may get confused and not respond to any of them.

To reinforce the behavior, practice calling your dog to you throughout the day, even when they're not expecting it. So, they could understand that coming when called is always a good thing.

And if your dog is particularly stubborn or easily distracted, you may need to work on their focus and attention skills before tackling the "come" command. Incorporating games and training exercises that require them to focus on you can help with this.

Heel

Have you ever tried taking your dog for a walk and ended up feeling like you were being dragged along instead? Many dog owners struggle with leash pulling and lack of control during walks. But fear not because today we will talk about the heel command and how it can help you achieve those peaceful, enjoyable walks you've been dreaming of.

So, what exactly is the heel command? Essentially, it's a command telling your dog to walk beside you on a loose leash. No pulling, no zigzagging, and definitely no chasing after squirrels. It's also a great command to teach your dog for safety reasons, as it can help you keep your dog away from potential dangers such as roads and other hazards.

Now, teaching your dog to the heel may seem like a daunting task, but with some patience and positive reinforcement, it can be done! One of the first things you'll want to do is choose a designated side for your dog to walk on. Most people prefer the left side, but ultimately, it's up to you. Once you've chosen your side, start practicing walking with your dog on a loose leash. Stop and wait for him to return to you when the dog begins to pull. Once they do, reward them with praise and a treat. Over time, your dog will learn that pulling doesn't get them anywhere, but staying by your side does.

Another important aspect of teaching your dog to heel is using the right timing and rewards. Reward your dog immediately when they're walking calmly beside you. This reinforces the behavior and lets them know they're doing something right.

Once your dog has mastered walking calmly on a loose leash, you can add the heel command. Simply say "heel" or your chosen command and guide your dog to your designated side. Again, reward him for staying by your side.

Leave it

Do you know how sometimes your pup gets into something they shouldn't, like your favorite shoes or that juicy steak you just cooked?
The "leave it" command is all about impulse control. It teaches your dog to resist the urge to grab something he wants and instead focus on you and the reward coming his way. It's a great way to prevent your dog from getting into dangerous situations or causing damage around the house.

To teach this command, first, find a treat your dog loves. Hold the treat in your closed hand and let your dog sniff and lick it. Say "leave it" in a firm but calm voice when your furry friend shows interest in the treat. Wait a few seconds, open your hand, and give your dog a different treat. This shows them that good things happen when they listen to the "leave it" command.

Once your dog has mastered leaving a treat in your closed hand, you can move on to leaving treats on the ground. Put a treat on the floor and cover it with your hand. Say "leave it" when your dog wants the treat and cover it again. When your dog backs away, offer him a different treat and praise.
Don't expect your dog to get the command right away – it takes time and practice. Gradually increase the difficulty of the exercise by leaving treats out in the open or tempting items on the counter. Apply positive reinforcement and recompense your dog when he do well.

To reinforce the "leave it" command, use it when your dog tries to grab something they shouldn't, like a sock or a shoe. Say "leave it" in a firm voice and then redirect your dog's attention to a toy or treat he can play with instead.

Down

Let's talk about "down" - not as in feeling down, but the command that tells your furry friend to lay down flat on the ground. It may seem like a simple command, but mastering "down" is essential for your dog's obedience and peace of mind.

"Down" is a great way to keep your dog under control in situations where they might get a little too excited. Maybe your dog gets too worked up when visitors come to your home, or perhaps they get too rowdy when you take them out for a walk. It lets your dog relax and stay calm by teaching him to lie down on command.

Now, teaching your dog to lie down isn't rocket science, but it requires patience and a lot of positive reinforcement. Start by getting your dog into the "sit" position. Hold a treat near your dog's nose when he sits and lowers the treat to the floor. As you do this, say "down" in a firm but gentle voice. Following the treat with their nose, the dog will lie down.
Praise and give him the treat when he lies down. Repeat this procedure daily until he gets the hang of it.

As your dog becomes more comfortable with "down," start using the command without the treat. You can still reward them with a treat once they've successfully laid down, but eventually, you'll want them to respond to the command alone.
We've learned about all the important commands to teach your furry friend. Next, we will work on getting you to understand what your dog is telling you with their body language.

Part 🐾3

Reading Between the Woofs: Understanding Dog Body Language and Behavior

Have you ever found yourself staring into your furry friend's eyes and wondering what they're really thinking? Do they love us as much as we love them, or are they secretly plotting to steal our snacks? Luckily that is a worry you can dispel from your mind soon because, in this part of the book, we will decode the mysteries of dog body language and behavior. From wagging tails to perked ears, we'll uncover the hidden messages our pups are trying to send us (spoiler alert: it's usually just "I love you, and I want belly rubs"). Get ready to do some pup-pup severe observation as you learn to read between the woofs!

Interpreting The Body Language

Dogs communicate a lot through their body language, and with a little bit of knowledge, you can learn to interpret what they're saying. Let's start with the basics. A dog's tail is one of the most expressive parts of his body, and it can tell you a lot about his feelings. When a dog feels happy and confident, his or her tail will be relaxed and wag loosely from side to side. However, if your dog's tail is stiff and pointed straight up, this could be a sign that he feels threatened or aggressive.

It's also important to pay attention to your dog's ears. When a dog is feeling relaxed, his ears will be in a neutral position. However, his ears might be flattened against his head if he is scared or anxious. And if he feels curious or alert, his ears might be perked up and pointed forward.
Another important aspect of a dog's body language is its facial expression. When a dog feels relaxed and happy, the mouth will be slightly open, and his or her tongue might hang out. However, if your dog's mouth is closed tightly and his lips are pulled back, this could be a sign that he's feeling threatened or aggressive.

Don't think that your dog is happy when its tail is wagging. While it's true that a loose, wagging tail usually indicates a happy dog, it's essential to pay attention to the rest of his body language as well. For example, if your dog's tail is wagging stiffly and his body is tense, this could be a sign that he's feeling fearful or aggressive.

It's also essential to remember that every dog is different, and their body language might mean something completely different from other dogs. For example, some dogs might naturally hold their tails higher than others, even when feeling relaxed and happy. Getting to know your dog's unique body language and what's normal for him is important.

In addition to interpreting your dog's body language, pay attention to your body language when interacting with your dog. Dogs are very attuned to human body language and can pick up on even subtle cues like changes in posture or facial expressions. So, if you're feeling anxious or nervous, your dog might pick up on that and become more anxious himself.

Using calming body language is one way to help your dog feel more relaxed and comfortable. This means keeping your body relaxed and loose, making gentle movements, and avoiding direct eye contact (which can be seen as threatening in dog language). By using calming body language yourself, you can help your dog feel more at ease and less stressed.

Of course, interpreting your dog's body language is just one part of the communication between you and your furry friend. It's also important to pay attention to his vocalizations, like barks and whines, and to understand his personality and behavior. For example, some dogs might be naturally more outgoing and sociable, while others might be more reserved and independent. By understanding your dog's unique personality and behavior, you can better communicate with him and provide him with the support and training he needs.

The context of your dog's behavior is also essential. For example, if your dog growls or barks when someone comes to the door, this could be a sign of protective behavior rather than aggression. By understanding the context of your dog's behavior, you can better respond to his needs and prevent potential misunderstandings.

Also, recognize when your dog is positively communicating with you. For example, if your dog wags his tail when you come home or snuggles up to you on the couch, this is a sign that he trusts and loves you. Responding to these positive signals helps strengthen your bond with your dog and improve your overall relationship.

Body language is just one piece of the puzzle when understanding your dog's emotions. In the next chapter, we'll dive deeper into the different moods dogs experience and how to recognize and respond to them.

Recognize And Understand Moods

Dogs can't speak English (or any other human language, for that matter), so it's up to us to pay attention to their body language and behavior to figure out what they're feeling. Dogs, like people, have a wide range of emotions. They can feel happy, sad, scared, angry, and everything else. And just like with people, it's not always easy to tell what a dog feels just by looking at them.

One of the most obvious ways to tell a dog's feelings is by looking at its tail. A wagging tail generally means a happy dog, but the speed and position of the wag can tell you more about its mood. A high, stiff tail wag can indicate excitement or agitation, while a low, slow wag can mean the dog feels relaxed or submissive. On the other hand, a tucked tail can be a sign of fear or anxiety.

It's essential to pay attention to dogs' ears. If a dog's ears are standing up and alert, it could mean they're excited or curious. Ears pinned back against the dog's head mean submission or fear. And if their ears are relaxed and slightly to the side, they feel content and relaxed.
Facial expressions can also be a good indicator of a dog's mood. A relaxed, open mouth can indicate a happy, relaxed dog, while a tense, closed mouth could mean they feel anxious or upset. And if a dog shows their teeth, it could be a sign of aggression or fear.

Make sure you're paying attention to your dog's overall posture. A confident, dominant dog will stand tall with his chest, and head held high, while a submissive dog might cower or lower their head. And if a dog feels anxious or scared, it might hunch its shoulders or tuck its tail between its legs.

With all that being said, you must also note that every dog is unique and that one dog's body language might differ from another. For example, some dogs might wag their tails when they're feeling anxious or nervous, while others might growl when they're playing.
So, knowing your dog, you will be careful of his particular cues.

One way to better recognize your dog's moods is to observe them more. Watch how they interact with other dogs and people and observe how they behave in different situations. And if you're ever unsure about your dog's feelings, don't be afraid to ask a professional for help. A veterinarian or dog trainer can help you better understand your dog's behavior and give you tips on responding to their moods.
Once you've better understood your dog's moods, you'll be better equipped to address some of the most common behavior problems. In the next chapter, we'll explore some of the most common issues dog owners face, and I'll provide tips and strategies for dealing with them.

Most Common Behavior Problems

Dogs are great companions, but sometimes they can be a bit of a handful. From barking at the mailman to chewing on your favorite shoes, dogs can develop all sorts of behavior problems that can drive even the most patient owner up the wall. In this chapter, we'll explore some of the most common behavior problems that dogs develop so we can tackle them efficiently and with as few issues as possible.

One of the most common issues that dog owners face is excessive barking. While barking is a natural behavior for dogs, it can become problematic when it's constant and disrupts your daily life. One way to address excessive barking is to identify the root cause. Does the dog break out of anxiety, boredom, or a desire for attention? At first, you must understand why he is barking. Then you must address the underlying issue. This might involve providing more exercise or mental stimulation, creating a safe space for your dog to retreat when they're anxious, or simply ignoring attention-seeking behavior.

Another common behavior problem is destructive chewing. Dogs love to chew, and it's perfectly normal for them to do so. However, when they start chewing on your furniture or other valuable items, it can become a major issue. To address destructive chewing, ensure your dog has plenty of appropriate chew toys and teach them what is and isn't acceptable to chew. You can also use deterrents like bitter apple spray to discourage them from chewing on non-toy items.

You may not like your dog dig! His behavior is natural, but he may destroy your garden. To address digging, ensure your dog has plenty of exercises and mental stimulation to keep them occupied. Choose an area of your garden where your dog might dig and reward him when he goes there.

Aggression is also common. Whether directed toward people or other dogs, aggression is a serious issue that should be addressed immediately. Working with a professional trainer or behaviorist can help address aggression, as they can help identify the root cause of the behavior and develop a plan for managing it.

Separation anxiety may be something you face as well. Dogs are social animals, and being alone for extended periods can be stressful. When your dog fell separation anxiety, he can bark loudly, whine, or soil the house. To address separation anxiety, start by gradually increasing the amount of time your dog spends alone and ensuring they have plenty of toys and treats to keep them occupied. Crate training may become comfortable when your dog is left alone at home.

Dealing with behavior problems can be challenging, but with patience, consistency, and some know-how, you can help your dog overcome even the most complex issues. However, it's also essential to prevent problems from arising in the first place by providing your dog with plenty of opportunities to socialize with other dogs and people. In the next chapter, we'll explore the importance of socialization and provide tips for helping your furry friend develop positive relationships with humans and other canines.

Socializing With Dogs and People

So, you've got a furry friend at home and want to ensure they're as happy and friendly as possible. Well, socializing is vital! It's like going to a party and knowing everyone there – the more comfortable and familiar you are with the people and dogs around you, the better time you'll have. So, let's dive into some tips and tricks for socializing your puppy!

First things first, start early. Puppies are like little sponges – they soak up everything around them, good and bad. So, the earlier you start socializing your pup, the better. Expose them to different people, dogs, and environments, like parks and cafes. Make sure they're up-to-date on their vaccinations before taking them out into the big wide world, though!

Next up, remember to go at your dog's pace. If your pup is shy or anxious around new people or dogs, don't force them into uncomfortable situations. Instead, take it slow and introduce them to new things gradually. Maybe start by inviting a friend with a calm dog over to your house and let your dog sniff and get used to them before going on walks or to the park.

Speaking of walks, they're a great way to socialize your dog. But be aware of their body language and reactions to other dogs. If they seem nervous or aggressive, keep your distance and redirect their attention to you with treats or toys. On the other hand, if they're calm and friendly, let them say hello and play with other dogs.

It's also important to teach your dog good manners around people. This includes not jumping up on strangers or pulling on the leash. Use positive reinforcement to encourage good behavior. And if your dog does make a mistake, be patient and redirect their attention to something more appropriate, like a toy.

But what about when you're introducing your dog to new people? Again, take it slow and let your dog approach the person on their terms. Encourage the person to crouch and let your dog sniff them rather than towering over them. And make sure the person knows not to pet your dog on the head, as this can be intimidating.

So, to sum it up: socializing is all about exposing your dog to different people, dogs, and environments safely and positively. Start at your dog's pace early and use positive reinforcement to encourage good behavior. And remember, every dog is unique – so don't compare your dog's progress to others. If you're putting in the effort to socialize your pup, you're doing great!

Even the most well-socialized dogs can sometimes develop bad habits because of mistakes the owner makes when training. In the next chapter, we'll explore some of the most common training mistakes and provide guidance on how to avoid them. By being aware of these pitfalls and taking a proactive approach to training, you can help your furry friend become the best version of themselves.

Mistake On Training

Training your furry best friend can be quite an adventure. Some dogs take to it like a fish to water, while others may take a little more coaxing. And then, of course, there's the occasional mistake that every dog owner makes along the way.

Consistency is key! You make a terrible mistake if you aren't consistent in the training! Imagine trying to learn a new language, but your teacher only shows up once a week and changes the lesson plan every time. That would be frustrating, right? Well, the same goes for your dog. If you only train them sporadically and change up the rules every time, they will get confused and frustrated.

Another common mistake is not being patient enough. I know you want your dog to be perfectly trained right now, but that's unrealistic. Training takes a lot of patience and time, and every dog is different. A dog picks up on things quickly, while another needs more time to understand. Take a deep breath and remember that your pup is learning at its own pace.

Speaking of patience, let's talk about punishment. Remember that dogs don't understand punishment in the same way that humans do. If your dog makes a mistake, punishing them isn't going to teach them what to do instead. In fact, it could make them fearful and anxious, which will only make training harder. Instead, try to redirect their behavior toward what you want them to do and reward them when they get it right.

Another mistake many dog owners make is insufficient mental and physical stimulation. Dogs need both to stay well and joyful; without it, they can become tired and devastated. Give your dog plenty of opportunities to play and exercise and try different types of toys and puzzles to keep their minds engaged.

Lastly, it's important to remember that every dog is an individual. What works for one may not work for another, and that's okay. Don't be afraid to try different training methods and techniques until you find what works best for you and your furry friend.

Making mistakes in training is a normal part of the learning process, but it's important to recognize when your dog may be struggling because of your error. This chapter has aided with that. In the next chapter, we'll explore some of the signs that your dog may be experiencing mental health issues and guide on when it's time to seek the advice of a veterinarian.

Mental Health and the Vet

Do you want your pets to be happy and healthy? After all, they're our constant companions and loyal confidantes. But sometimes, despite our best efforts, our pups may experience mental health issues or require veterinary care. As a responsible pet owner, you should learn to recognize the signs and seek professional help when needed.

One of the most common mental health issues in dogs is anxiety. Your dog can experience feelings of anxiety and stress, exactly like you. Common signs of anxiety in dogs include excessive barking, destructive behavior, and aggression toward people or other animals. If you notice these behaviors in your pup, consult your veterinarian to determine the best course of treatment. They may recommend behavior modification techniques or medication to help manage your dog's anxiety.

Another common mental health issue in dogs is depression. Signs of depression in dogs can include lethargy, loss of appetite, and decreased interest in activities they once enjoyed. This can result from a significant life change, such as losing a companion or a medical issue. Again, consult your veterinarian to determine the underlying cause of your dog's depression and develop a treatment plan.

In addition to mental health issues, our furry friends may also require veterinary care for physical health issues. Periodically seeing a veterinarian is essential to identify any health issues early on and prevent them from becoming graver. Dental care is also necessary, as untreated dental problems can run into other health problems.

Also, keep up with your dog's vaccinations and preventative care, such as flea and tick prevention. This can help protect your dog from common illnesses and diseases and keep them safe from parasites.

Our furry friends may not always be able to communicate their needs to us. It's up to us dog owners to be vigilant and recognize any signs of distress or illness. By providing regular mental and physical health care for our pups, we can ensure they live long, happy, and healthy lives.

Taking care of your dog's physical and mental health is essential. You can promote dogs' mental health by playing with and stimulating them. In the next part of the book, we'll explore the world of dog toys and treats, providing recommendations for products that can keep your furry friend engaged, entertained, and mentally stimulated.

Part 🐾4

Toys and Treats:
Finding the Right Playthings for Your Pup

Are you tired of your pup turning your shoes into chew toys? Would you like to discover many ideas for keeping your pet amused and out of trouble? Well, fear not because, in this part, we will talk about one of every dog's favorite thing - toys and treats! From squeaky balls to puzzle toys, we'll explore the world of dog playthings and find the perfect match for your pup's personality. Plus, we'll even dive into the world of homemade toys, so you can flex your DIY skills and impress your furry friend with your crafting abilities. Hoist the anchor because we're about to sail on a journey to find the perfect toys and treats for your furry first mate!

Right Toys

The one thing that makes our furry friends go absolutely bonkers? Toys! Toys can entertain your dog and have a ton of benefits for him. From providing mental stimulation to promoting physical exercise, toys are essential to a happy and healthy dog's life.

Just like how we humans have different preferences when it comes to our favorite things, dogs also have unique tastes in toys. But not all toys are created equal. In this chapter, we'll explore how to choose suitable toys for your dog, so you can keep them entertained and engaged for hours on end.

Types of Dog Toys

There are so many different types of toys out there for us dogs to play with that it can be hard to decide which ones it's best to sink their teeth into. But I'm here to give you the lowdown on the different types of toys and their benefits (and maybe a few drawbacks).

First up, we have chew toys. These are great for dogs who love to gnaw on things (and, honestly, that's most of them). You can buy chew toys like bones, strings, or rubber. They can help keep dogs' teeth clean and healthy and are also great for relieving stress and anxiety.

Next, we have interactive toys. These toys require dogs to do something to get a reward, like a treat or a toy that dispenses food. These toys are great for keeping their minds sharp and preventing boredom, which can lead to destructive behavior. They're also a fun way to encourage bonding between humans and dogs.

Puzzle toys are another type of interactive toy that are designed to challenge dogs' problem-solving skills. These toys usually have hidden compartments or treats that they have to figure out how to get to. They're good for keeping them mentally active and help prevent older cognitive decline.

Fetch toys are a classic favorite for many dogs. They come in all shapes and sizes, from tennis balls to frisbees to sticks (although, let's be clear, sticks are not always safe for dogs to play with). Fetch toys are great for exercising, burning off energy, and bonding with your pup.

Finally, we have plush toys. These soft, stuffed toys can provide some dogs comfort and security. They're not as durable as other types of toys, so they may not be the best choice for dogs who like to chew. But for dogs who just want something to snuggle with, plush toys can be a great option.

Choosing Toys for Your Dog

With so many different types of toys, how do you choose the right ones for your pup? Don't worry; I'll explain how to do it. At the outset, consider your dog's age, size, breed, and personality. For example, a small, gentle toy poodle might not be interested in a giant chew toy for a Great Dane. And a high-energy Border Collie might need more interactive toys to stimulate their busy brain.

Next, consider the materials of the toys. Some dogs love the feel of plush toys, while others prefer tougher rubber or nylon toys that can stand up to their powerful jaws. If your dog is an aggressive chewer, you'll want to look for toys labeled as "indestructible" or "heavy-duty."

When introducing new toys to your dog, make it a fun and positive experience. Play with the toy yourself to show your dog that it's something worth getting excited about. You can also try rubbing the toy with some peanut butter or another tasty treat to make it more appealing.

And remember, always supervise your dog when playing with toys to ensure they don't accidentally swallow something they shouldn't. So go ahead and spoil your furry friend with some new toys, but always prioritize their safety and enjoyment.

Safe Toys for Dogs

You know how we all have that one friend who eats anything and everything they can get their paws on? Well, that friend can be a lot like our furry companions regarding toys. Choosing safe toys for our dogs is important so they don't end up in the vet's office with an upset stomach or worse.

Choosing a toy for your pet, consider their chewing habits. Do they have a habit of tearing things apart and eating the pieces? If so, avoid toys with small parts that your dog could unintentionally eat. Trust me; you don't want to spend your weekend at the animal hospital waiting for a toy to pass through your dog's digestive system.

Another thing to watch out for is toxic materials. Some toys can be made with harmful chemicals that can be dangerous to our dogs. Check the label to ensure that the materials used to make the toy are non-toxic and safe for dogs.

Consider choosing a toy with the right size for your furry friend. Your dog could unintentionally eat a too-small toy and be unable to play with a too-large toy. The packaging or label should provide information on the appropriate size for your dog.

Finally, watch your dog's toys for signs of wear and tear. If a toy starts to fall apart, it's time to retire it and get a new one. So, you can prevent your furry friend from ingesting small pieces or potentially dangerous materials.

We must make safe choices for him. By choosing safe toys for our dogs, we can help them stay healthy, happy, and entertained.

Maintaining and Replacing Dog Toys

We all know how much our furry friends adore their toys, but sometimes we forget to keep them in good condition. It's important to keep their toys in good shape to avoid any accidents or health issues. So, let's talk about maintaining and replacing dog toys!

Cleaning is crucial! Would you want to play with a dirty, smelly toy? Of course not! So, take some time to clean your dog's toys. Soft toys can be machine-washed or hand-washed with mild detergent. Hard toys can be wiped down with a damp cloth and mild soap. And for those toys that get a little funky, try using a mixture of vinegar and water to disinfect them. After washing the toys, you must rinse them off carefully.

No toy is indestructible, and as much as we'd like to believe our furry friends are gentle creatures, they can tear through a toy in minutes. So, you must check their toys regularly for any damage or signs of wear and tear. If a toy starts falling apart, it's time to replace it.

Replacing toys isn't just for the sake of your dog's entertainment; it's also for their safety. If your dog has managed to rip apart a toy and is now exposed to stuffing, small parts, or dangerous materials, it's time to say goodbye to that toy. Also, dogs can get bored with toys, just like humans. So, turn their toys every week to keep them curious.

You might think, "But my dog has a favorite toy they love to death!" I get it; I really do. But even the best-loved toys need to be retired eventually. So, if your dog's favorite toy looks worse for wear, it's time to say goodbye. But don't worry. There are plenty of new toys out there waiting for your pup to discover.

Now that we've covered the importance of choosing the right toys for your furry friend let's explore another fun and creative option: homemade toys! If you're looking for a way to entertain your pup while saving a bit of money, homemade toys can be a great option. With just a few simple materials and a bit of imagination, you can create toys that are just as enjoyable and stimulating for your dog as store-bought ones. So, grab some supplies, turn to the next chapter, and get ready to make some paw-some toys for your furry friend!

Homemade Toys

This chapter will explore the wonderful world of DIY dog toys. Not only are homemade toys often more affordable than store-bought ones, but they're also a great way to bond with your dog and stimulate their mind. Plus, you get to show off your artistic skills to your pup - what's not to love? We'll discuss different types of homemade toys you can make with items you may already have lying around your house. I've covered you, from repurposing old t-shirts to transforming old water bottles into fun playthings. So, let's roll up our sleeves and get to crafting!

Materials for Making Homemade Toys

Are you ready to unleash your inner DIY guru and create homemade toys for your furry friend? Then you first need to raid your closets and see what kind of materials you have on hand that can be transformed into fun toys for your dog. Have some old t-shirts or socks that have seen better days? Don't throw them away just yet! They can be repurposed into tug toys or even a simple "snuffle mat" for your dog to search for treats. Tennis balls can be sliced open and stuffed with treats for a fun game of fetch, and rope can be knotted together for a game of tug-of-war.

But don't limit yourself to just these materials - get creative! Have an old plastic water bottle lying around? Wrap it in a t-shirt and tie the ends for a crunchy noise-making toy. Or cut an old fleece blanket into strips to create a braided tug toy. The possibilities are endless!
Of course, you must ensure that any materials you use are safe for your dog. Avoid materials that can be easily shredded or swallowed, such as small plastic bits or stuffing from old pillows. And if you're not sure if a material is safe, err on the side of caution and skip it.
Now that you've got some ideas for materials, it's time to let your imagination run wild and see what kind of toys you can create for your dog!

DIY Chew Toys

Are you tired of spending a fortune on dog toys that your furry friend chews up in minutes? Well, why not make your DIY chew toys? Not only will you save money, but you'll also have the satisfaction of knowing you made the toy yourself. Plus, you'll be repurposing old clothes, which is a win-win for you and the environment.

One of the easiest DIY chew toys to make is the t-shirt rope toy. All you need is an old t-shirt and a pair of scissors. Simply cut the t-shirt into thin strips and tie them together to form a long rope. Then, braid the rope together tightly and tie the ends together. Voila! You have a chew toy that your dog will love.

Another option is the sock ball toy. All you need is an old sock and a tennis ball. Place the tennis ball inside the sock and tie a knot at the end. You can make it even more exciting by adding a squeaker or stuffing the sock with treats.

One of the benefits of DIY chew toys is that you can customize them to your dog's size and chewing strength. For example, if you have a heavy chewer, you can make a rope toy with multiple strands of t-shirt strips to make it more durable. You can also adjust the size of the sock ball toy by using a bigger or smaller sock and tennis ball. Another benefit of DIY chew toys is controlling the materials used.

DIY Puzzle Toys

Save some money while also providing mental stimulation for your pup with DIY puzzle toys using common household items. You can create the classic cardboard box puzzle. So, get a few treats, scissors, and a cardboard box. Place treats inside the box and cut holes in its sides. Your dog must use their problem-solving skills to determine how to get the treats out.

Next, we have the PVC pipe puzzle. You'll need some PVC pipes of varying lengths, a saw, and some treats. Cut the pipes into different lengths and place treats inside. Then, cap off one end of each pipe and let your dog figure out how to get the treats from the other end.

Creating the plastic bottle puzzle is also an option. This one is super easy and only requires a plastic bottle, some treats, and scissors. Place treats inside the bottle and cut a few holes in its side. Your furry friend must figure out how to shake the bottle to gain these delicious treats.

DIY Fetch Toys

Fetch is one of the classic dog games everyone loves playing with furry friends. But what if you could take that game to the next level with homemade fetch toys? You don't need to be a craft expert to make a DIY fetch toy. All you need are some simple materials like tennis balls, rope, and old socks. With a little creativity and effort, you can create unique and entertaining toys your dog will love playing with.

To start, take an old sock and stuff a tennis ball inside. Tie a knot at the end to secure the ball, and voila! You have a brand-new fetch toy. You can also use a rope to create a tug-of-war style toy by knotting two pieces of rope together and braiding them into a thicker, sturdier toy.

If you're feeling more adventurous, try making a fetch stick using a long piece of wood, a tennis ball, and some strong glue. Simply drill a hole through the center of the wood, insert the ball, and glue it in place. Your dog will love chasing after this unique and handmade toy.

DIY Interactive Toys

Picture this: your dog is bored out of their mind, pacing around the house and whining for attention. You've tried every store-bought toy in the book, but nothing seems to capture their interest for more than a few minutes. What's a responsible and loving dog owner to do? Get crafty with some DIY interactive toys, of course!

Not only are these toys easy and inexpensive to make, but they also provide a great mental workout for your furry friend. By requiring your dog to problem-solve for a reward, interactive toys can keep them engaged and entertained for much longer than your average squeaky toy. Plus, the satisfaction you'll get from watching your pup work hard to earn their treats is truly priceless.

So, what are some materials you'll need for these interactive toys? You likely already have most of them lying around the house! Cardboard boxes are a popular choice for creating hiding spots and puzzle pieces, while treats like peanut butter and carrots can be used to entice your dog to play. You may also want to invest in PVC pipes or sturdy plastic containers to create more complex puzzles.

Once you've gathered your materials, the possibilities for interactive toys are endless. You could create a simple "find the treat" game by hiding treats in cardboard boxes and having your dog sniff them out, or you could get more elaborate with a puzzle box that requires your dog to push or slide objects in a certain sequence to reveal a hidden treat. So, give your creativity free rein! You can customize the toys to your dog's preferences and abilities, ensuring they'll never get bored playing with them.

Safety Considerations

It's great that you're considering making homemade toys for your furry friend. Not only is it a fun and creative activity, but it's also a great way to save money and reduce waste. But before rummaging through your junk drawer for materials, let's discuss safety considerations. After all, we don't want your pup to end up in the doggy ER because of a DIY toy gone wrong.

First and foremost, avoiding any materials that can be easily swallowed or choked on is important. This includes small buttons, beads, or other small parts that can break off or be pulled off the toy. Additionally, be cautious when using materials that can splinter or break easily, such as certain types of wood or plastic.

It's also important to use non-toxic materials. This means avoiding any materials that could potentially be harmful if ingested by your pup, such as certain types of paint or glue. Stick to natural, food-safe materials whenever possible. Lastly, be mindful of the size and strength of your dog when choosing materials for their toys.

But don't worry. Making homemade toys for your dog can still be safe and fun with a little bit of caution and creativity. If you're mindful of potential hazards and choose your materials wisely, your pup will have a blast playing with their new toys. Happy crafting!

Congratulations! You've just become a DIY master by learning how to make homemade toys for your furry friend. But why stop making toys when you can do so many other fun activities with your dog? In the next chapter, we'll explore the world of physical activities that you and your pup can enjoy together. We'll cover all those kinds of games.

Outdoor Physical Activity

The following few questions are directed at your furry friend. Are you feeling a bit sluggish lately? Has your human being telling you to get off the couch and exercise? Put yourself in your doggy's shoes. What would be the answers to these questions? Fear not if these answers are not favorable because, in this chapter, we'll be talking all about physical activities for dogs!

Regular physical exercise can do wonders for your dog's health and happiness. It can reduce stress and anxiety and even help prevent health issues like obesity and diabetes. This is an excellent way to bond with your furry friends. Of course, all kinds of emotional ties will be formed as your dog shows off his impressive skills.

In this chapter, we'll cover all the different types of outdoor physical activities you and your dog can enjoy together. Whether you have a high-energy pup who loves to run or a more laid-back dog who prefers a stroll, there's something for every pup.
Let's dive into the world of physical activities that dogs can enjoy outside!

Walks and Hikes

Ah, the great outdoors! The sights, the smells, the endless possibilities for adventure. For dogs, a walk or hike is more than just a chance to stretch their legs. It's an opportunity to explore the world around them, to soak up new experiences, and to bond with their humans.

Regarding physical activity, few things beat a good walk or hike. Not only does it provide essential exercise, but it's also great for a dog's mental health. Walking and hiking can help reduce stress and anxiety, promote socialization, and provide mental stimulation as they take in all the sights, sounds, and smells around them.

You must choose the right leash and harness to ensure your furry friend gets the most out of their walks and hikes. Different dogs have different needs, so make sure to take into account their size, strength, and temperament when selecting gear. Consider using a no-pull harness or a head halter if your dog is a strong puller. A simple leash and collar may be all you need if they're more laid back.
Of course, walks and hikes can get a little boring if they're always the same. To keep your dog engaged and motivated, mix things up by choosing new routes, exploring different terrain, or even

trying a new sport like geocaching or orienteering. Just keep safety in mind, and avoid areas with known hazards like steep drop-offs or dangerous wildlife. With the right gear and a little creativity, walks and hikes can be a highlight of your dog's day. So, grab your leash, lace up your boots, and hit the trail with your furry best friend in tow!

Running and Jogging

Have you ever seen a dog running at full speed, tongue out, ears flopping, just pure joy on its face? It's a beautiful thing, not just for the dog but for the human. Running or jogging with your dog can be a great bonding experience and provide some serious health benefits for both of you.

First, running and jogging help dogs maintain a healthy weight, just like humans do. It also helps strengthen their muscles and bones, which is especially important for breeds prone to hip dysplasia or other joint problems. Plus, running releases endorphins, improving a dog's mood and reducing anxiety.

But before you grab your sneakers and leash, there are a few things to keep in mind. First, make sure your dog is physically ready for running or jogging. Like you, your furry friend needs to build up his endurance progressively. Begin with slower and short walks, and gradually increment intensity and time every week.

Secondly, consider your dog's breed and individual needs. For example, short-nosed breeds like pugs and bulldogs may have trouble breathing during extended exercise, so running might not be the best option for them. On the other hand, some breeds, like greyhounds, are natural runners and may need more intense exercise to burn off their energy.

When you do start running with your dog, keep them safe. Ensure they are appropriately leashed and wearing a well-fitting harness rather than just a collar. This will help prevent any neck injuries from pulling or sudden stops. Also, pay attention to humidity and temperature. Dogs are more prone to heatstroke than humans, so avoid running in extreme heat or humidity.

Finally, don't forget to make it fun! Dogs love to explore and sniff, so let them lead the way (within reason, of course). Take breaks to play or just enjoy the scenery together. It's a great way to bond with your dog and get some exercise at the same time.

Swimming and Water Activities

It's time to dive into the wonderful world of swimming and water activities for dogs. While not all pups are natural-born swimmers, getting your furry friend into the water has plenty of benefits. Let's take a closer look, shall we?

Swimming is a great low-impact exercise option for dogs, making it ideal for those with joint problems or injuries. It provides a full-body workout, building strength, and endurance while being easy on the joints. Plus, it's a great way to cool off on hot summer days!

If your pooch isn't a natural swimmer, don't worry – there are plenty of ways to introduce them to the water. Start slowly, with shallow water and a life vest if needed. Encourage them with treats and positive reinforcement and supervise them closely at all times. Before you know it, they'll be paddling around like a pro!

Once your dog is comfortable in the water, plenty of fun activities exist. Fetch is a classic option, with the added challenge of retrieving toys from the water. You can also try swimming races with you or another dog as the competition. If you're feeling adventurous, dog-friendly water sports like dock diving and paddleboarding exist!

Of course, safety should always be a top priority when it comes to water activities. Ensure your dog wears a properly fitted life vest, and never leave them unattended in or near the water. Keep an eye out for signs of exhaustion or distress and be prepared to intervene if needed.

Agility Training

Agility training is not for the faint of heart - it's a full-blown, adrenaline-fueled obstacle course that will put you and your furry friend to the test. If you're going to start agility training with your furry friend, you're going to need some gear. This might sound intimidating but trust me, this equipment will make the whole experience more fun for you and your pup.

First up, we've got jumps. No, not the kind you do with your car, silly. We're talking about the kind of jumps that your dog can leap over. You can get different types of jumps, from simple, low hurdles to more advanced, higher jumps that'll make your dog feel like a true champion.

Next, we've got tunnels. Think of these like doggy wormholes. Your pup will love racing through them, giving them the feeling that they're on some kind of epic adventure. You can choose the best tunnel for your dog because there are tunnels in different sizes and shapes.

Weave poles are another piece of gear that you'll need. Your dog has to weave these poles in and out like they're doing some kind of fancy footwork. It's an excellent exercise for your pup's brain and body.

And let's not forget the A-frame, dog walk, and seesaw obstacles. These are mini versions of human parkour courses, and your dog will feel like a real-life superhero as they jump, balance, and climb through them.
Of course, you'll need something to mark out the course, so you can use cones, flags, or other markers to indicate where your dog should go.

If you feel crafty, you can make some of this equipment yourself. For example, you can make weave poles out of PVC pipes or use old tires to create jumps. Just do your research and use materials that are safe for your pup.

Alright, so you've decided to get your furry friend started with agility training. Great decision! But where do you even begin? Here are some tips to get your pup on the path to agility success:

- **Step 1**: Assess your dog's current physical fitness. Are they couch potatoes, or do they have some stamina? Agility training can be demanding, so your pup must be up for the challenge. Agility training can be physically demanding on your dog, so ensuring they are in good health and have no pre-existing injuries before starting is crucial. And don't forget to include proper warm-up and cool-down exercises before and after each training session to prevent injury.

- **Step 2**: Gather some equipment. No, you don't need to go out and buy expensive agility equipment right away. You can start with simple household items like chairs, broomsticks, and hula hoops. Get creative and make your obstacles!

- **Step 3**: Start with basic training. You can start by teaching your dog "sit," "stay," and other basic commands. These commands will come in handy when you're trying to get your dog to wait at the start line or stay on the contact obstacles.

- **Step 4**: Get your dog to try the distinct obstacles one at a time. Let them sniff and explore the obstacle before you attempt to get them to climb or jump over it. Use positive reinforcement and give them some treats to stimulate them to finish the block.

- **Step 5**: String the obstacles together into a sequence. Start with a simple sequence of just a few obstacles and gradually add more as your pup gets more comfortable and confident.

- **Step 6**: Make it fun! Agility training must be an amusement and formative experience for you and your furry friend. Toys, delicious treats, and praise make your dog more involved and motivated.

Remember, agility training takes time and patience. Don't expect your dog to become a pro overnight. But with consistency and practice, you and your furry friend can have a blast navigating an obstacle course together. Who knows, you might even become the next agility power duo!

Playtime with Other Dogs

A dog park is a place where furry friends can run, play, and sniff each other's butts to their heart's content. As a dog owner, there's nothing like watching your pup bounce around excitedly as they meet new friends and play games. But as much fun as it is to watch your dog play with other canines, it's important to do so safely. You don't want your pup getting hurt or getting into a fight.

That's where this section on playtime with other dogs comes in. We'll cover everything you need to know to keep your dog safe and happy while playing with other pups. First, let's discuss the benefits of socialization and playtime with other dogs. Dogs are social animals that grow on interaction with others. Regular playtime with other dogs can help them build confidence, learn how to communicate with other dogs, and even improve their overall behavior.
But not all playmates are created equal. When choosing other dogs for your pup to play with, consider their temperament, size, and play style. For example, a small, timid dog may not enjoy playing with a larger, boisterous dog.

It's also important to supervise playtime to prevent any aggressive behavior. Keep an eye on your dog's body language and step in if things start to get too rough. And if you notice any aggressive behavior from another dog, it's best to remove your pup from the situation.
So how can you find safe playmates for your dog? Dog parks can be a great place to start, but it's important to choose a well-maintained park with separate areas for small and large dogs. Why don't you contact other city dog owners to plan some playdates? It might be exciting and fun!
During playtime, bring along some toys to keep the dogs engaged and help prevent potential conflicts. But be sure to monitor the toys to ensure they're not causing possessive behavior.

Playtime with other dogs can be a wonderful way to keep your pup socialized and happy. Just remember to choose safe playmates, supervise playtime, and keep an eye on your dog's behavior. With a little bit of effort, you and your furry friend can enjoy many happy hours of playtime with other dogs.

Exercise for Senior Dogs

Some of our furry friends have grey hairs, less energy, and more wisdom. They may not be up for running marathons or jumping through hoops anymore, but that doesn't mean they should sit on the couch all day. Like humans, exercise is important for senior dogs to maintain a healthy body and mind. But before starting any new exercise regimen for your senior dog, consult their vet. They can help determine any underlying health issues or conditions that need to be considered. Once you have the green light, discover some tips to keep your senior dog grooving and moving.

Low-impact exercises are essential. This includes walks, gentle hikes, and even swimming if they enjoy it. The goal is to increase their heart rate but not overexert them. Shorter, more frequent walks may be more beneficial than one long walk.

Yoga isn't just for humans anymore. Yes, you heard me right. Yoga for dogs is a thing, and it can be an excellent option for senior dogs. It's low-impact, gentle on joints, and can help improve flexibility and balance.

Keeping your senior pet mentally stimulated and physically active is essential. Puzzle or treat-dispensing toys can keep their minds engaged and provide a bit of a workout.

If your senior dog is up for it, training sessions can be a great way to keep their mind sharp and bond with them. This could be as simple as practicing basic obedience commands or learning new tricks.

Watch for any signs of discomfort or exhaustion during exercise. If your senior dog shows signs of fatigue, it's time to stop and take a break. Keeping your senior dog hydrated is also essential, so bring water and a bowl with you on any outings.

Lastly, don't forget about the power of massage. Senior dogs can benefit greatly from gentle massages to improve circulation and reduce any aches and pains they may be experiencing.

After all that outdoor exercise, it's time for some fun indoor activities! But don't worry. We're not just going to sit around and be couch potatoes. We're going to keep our furry friends active and engaged with some exciting indoor activities both indoors. So, let's put on our thinking caps and get creative because the fun is about to begin!

Indoor Physical Activities

Watching your furry pal nap all day and not getting any exercise is disheartening. Do you want to keep them entertained even when the weather is not on your side? Well, you're in the right place! In this chapter, we'll talk about unique indoor activities for your dogs that will keep them busy and improve their physical and mental health.

We all know that dogs love to play and stay active, but sometimes outdoor activities are impossible. Maybe it's too cold or rainy outside, or you don't have a backyard or a nearby dog park. But that doesn't mean you can't have fun with your dog! Indoor activities are a great way to stimulate your dog's senses, burn off some energy, and teach them new tricks.

So, let's get started and explore some fun and unique indoor activities for your furry friend!

Dog Yoga

Are you ready to embark on a journey of relaxation and bonding with your furry friend? Let's talk about dog yoga! You might be wondering what dog yoga is. You can try new yoga poses with your dog and relax with him! It is a great way to bond with your furry friend and provides a variety of physical and mental benefits for you and your pup.

One of the main benefits of dog yoga is relaxation. Like humans, dogs can benefit from calming activities that help them reduce stress and anxiety. Practicing yoga poses with your dog can help you relax and unwind, creating a peaceful atmosphere in your home.

But that's not all - dog yoga can also help with physical fitness. Many poses involve stretching and gentle movements that can improve your dog's flexibility and mobility. Plus, it's a great way to get some exercise and burn off energy indoors when the weather outside is less than ideal.

So, how do you get started with dog yoga? The first step is to find a comfortable and quiet space in your home where you and your dog can practice together. You might want to invest in a yoga mat or blanket to provide a soft surface for your pup to lie on.

Next, it's time to start practicing some poses. Some popular dog yoga poses include the downward dog, the upward dog, and the triangle pose. Don't be afraid; I will provide instructions on how to perform these dog yoga poses.

First up, we have the downward dog. It's a classic yoga pose, and dogs do it all the time naturally. Start with your pup in a tabletop position with their hands and knees on the ground. Then, slowly lift their hips so that their back forms a "V" shape. Their head should be relaxed and hanging down. If your dog struggles to keep their paws flat on the ground, you can use treats to encourage them to relax their muscles.

Next is the upward dog. It's a great pose to stretch out the belly and chest muscles. Have your pup start by lying down on its belly. Then, with their paws still on the ground, lift their chest toward the ceiling while keeping their legs and hips on the ground. This pose is especially great for older dogs with stiff joints or arthritis.

Finally, we have the triangle pose. This is a bit challenging pose, but it's a great way to work on balance and coordination with your pup. Start with your dog standing up straight, then step one foot forward so they are in a lunge position. Then, have them reach one paw toward the sky while the other is planted firmly on the ground. Doing every pose, pay attention to your friend's body language, and don't force him to continue if he seems uncomfortable or can't maintain that pose.

In addition to practicing yoga poses with your dog, you can incorporate meditation and breathing exercises into your routine. These can help you and your dog relax and focus on the present moment.

Indoor Obstacle Course

Are you tired of the same old routine of fetching and walking with your furry friend? Do you want to give them a unique and challenging activity to stimulate them physically and mentally? Then, you and your pup might just need an indoor obstacle course.

An indoor obstacle course comprises different obstacles your dog has to navigate through, such as tunnels, jumps, weave poles, and more. This activity provides your dog with a challenge that can improve their coordination, balance, and problem-solving skills.

One of the best parts of an indoor obstacle course is that it can be set up in the comfort of your own home. All you need is space, household items, and a willing pup. Start by creating a plan for the course and decide on the obstacles you want to include.

If you're stumped on ideas to create an indoor obstacle course for your pup, let me help. First, clear out some space in your living room (or any other room with enough space), so your dog has plenty of room to run around. Next, gather some items around the house that can be used as obstacles. You can use pillows to create a tunnel, chairs to jump over, and even cardboard boxes to weave through.

To create the tunnel, simply stack a few pillows together in a row and make a small opening at one end. Your dog can then run through the tunnel to the other side.

Place a chair or two in a row for the jumping obstacle and encourage your dog to jump over them. Chairs may be sturdy and must stay upright!

Set up a series of cardboard boxes in a zigzag pattern for the weaving obstacle. Ensure enough space between the boxes for your dog to navigate through them. You can also place some treats at the end of the weaving obstacle to encourage your dog to complete the course.

Now, let's talk about the benefits of an indoor obstacle course for your dog. It provides a physical and mental workout to help them maintain their physical fitness and mental sharpness. It can also help strengthen the bond between you and your furry friend as you work together to navigate the course. This exciting activity can discourage destructive behavior and reduce boredom.

When setting up the course, start with easy obstacles and gradually increase the difficulty level as your dog becomes more comfortable and confident. Utilize daily rewards and positive reinforcement to encourage and motivate your furry friend. Treats, toys, and lots of praise can go a long way in keeping your dog engaged and focused on the task at hand.

Tricks and Training

Training and teaching your dog new tricks can be a great way to provide mental stimulation for your furry friend. Let's start with some tips on training and teaching tricks to your dog indoors.

To start, choose the right time and environment for training. Ensure your dog is relaxed before each training session. Pick a quiet spot in your home where you and your dog can focus without distractions.

Next, it's important to choose a reward that your dog loves. Whether it's a treat or a favorite toy, make sure it's something that your dog is willing to work for. So your dog will be more motivated during training.

Start with the basics when teaching a new trick, and work your way up. For example, if you're teaching your dog to shake, start by rewarding them for lifting their paw off the ground. Once they've mastered this, you can add the verbal cue "shake" and reward them for raising their paw when you say it.

Be patient and consistent during training. Dogs learn best through repetition, so be prepared to practice the same trick multiple times. Keep training sessions short and sweet, around 10 to 15 minutes at a time. This will help keep your dog focused and prevent them from getting bored.

You can add more difficult tricks as your dog becomes more comfortable with training. Still, always keep it positive and fun for your dog. If they become frustrated or tired, take a break and try again later.

Even indoors, having a blast with our furry friends is possible. Once, you may not have the energy for a play session. That's where mental exercises come in handy! Just like us humans, our dogs need to exercise their brains to stay healthy and happy. So, in the next chapter, we'll explore some fun and challenging ways to keep your pup's mind sharp, whether you're lounging at home or out and about. Get ready to put on your thinking cap. Don't forget to put on your dog's, too!

Mental Exercises

Ready to exercise your brain a bit? Well, right now, we're not talking about human brains. We're talking about dog brains! That's right, our furry friends need mental exercise, too! It's just as important as physical exercise. Mental exercises help keep our dog's brain healthy and sharp, just like how solving puzzles or playing games keeps our human brains active and engaged.

Just like how we humans can get bored and restless if we don't have anything to keep our minds occupied, dogs can also become anxious and destructive without mental stimulation. We can help prevent problem behaviors and improve their overall well-being by providing our dogs with opportunities to use their brainpower. So, if you're ready to become a doggie brain trainer, you've come to the right place! In this chapter, we'll cover some fun and unique ways to exercise your dog's mind, keeping them entertained and engaged while also strengthening their cognitive abilities.

Now that we've established the importance of mental exercise let's dive into the types of exercises we'll cover in this chapter. From interactive puzzle toys to scent games and obedience training, there are plenty of ways to challenge your dog's mind and keep them entertained. So, let's get started!

Enrichment Toys

Look no further than enrichment toys for a great way to stimulate your furry friend's mind. These toys are designed to provide mental stimulation and help alleviate boredom in dogs.
Enrichment toys come in all shapes and sizes. Some are designed to dispense treats, while others require dogs to solve puzzles or manipulate objects to access rewards. They can be made from plastic, wood, rubber, and other materials.
The benefits of enrichment toys are numerous. They can help prevent destructive behavior, reduce anxiety, and promote mental wellness. In this way, you can interact with your dog with fun.

When choosing an enrichment toy for your dog, consider its size, breed, and personality. Some toys are designed specifically for small dogs or breeds with strong chewing tendencies. Others may be better suited for dogs who enjoy puzzles and challenges.

Supervising your dog when playing with enrichment toys is important, especially if they're new to the toy or tend to be aggressive chewers. And don't forget to wash and inspect the toy regularly to ensure it's still safe and functional.

Interactive Feeding

The mealtime routine for your furry best friend can become quite boring, with the same actions repeated daily. The puppy would likely appreciate it if you spice things up and give them a challenge. Interactive feeding allows you to add that variety.

Interactive feeding is a great way to provide mental stimulation for your dog while also making mealtime more enjoyable. It's like a fun puzzle for them to solve, and who doesn't love a good puzzle? Plus, it can help prevent boredom and damaging behaviors, like chewing on your favorite shoes or tearing apart your couch cushions.

There are a variety of ways to make feeding interactive. One option is to use puzzle feeders, specially designed toys that require your dog to work for their food. These toys usually have hidden compartments or obstacles your dog has to navigate to access the food.

Another option is to use a snuffle mat, which is a mat with lots of small pockets or crevices where you can hide kibble or treats. Your dog then has to use their sense of smell to find the food, which is great mental stimulation.

You can also use a treat-dispensing toy, which releases food as your dog plays with it. These toys usually have a small opening or hole where food can come out, and your dog has to figure out how to manipulate the toy to get the food.

When choosing an interactive feeding method, deliberate your dog's individual needs and abilities. For example, if your dog is a heavy chewer, select a puzzle feeder that can withstand its strong jaws. If your dog is a senior or has limited mobility, a snuffle mat may be better than a more physically demanding puzzle feeder.

It's also important to start slowly and ensure your dog understands the game. Some dogs may need more guidance than others, so be patient and provide plenty of positive reinforcement as they figure it out. You can start using a simple puzzle feeder or treat-dispensing toy and gradually increase the difficulty as your dog becomes more comfortable.

Interactive feeding can be a great addition to your dog's daily routine, providing mental stimulation and helping to prevent boredom and destructive behaviors. So, next time you're tempted to dump your dog's food in a boring old bowl, think outside the box and try interactive feeding!

Obedience Training

If the doggo is being a little bit too rambunctious, have no fear because obedience training is here to the rescue! You can involve your dog's mind and offer mental stimulation through obedience training. Plus, it's an excellent opportunity to bond with your four-legged companion. Here you will learn what obedience training is.

Let's chat about the benefits of obedience training first. Not only can it improve your dog's behavior, but it can also boost their confidence and give them a sense of accomplishment. It could provide mental stimulation, and your dog will be less bored. Win-win!

You can teach your dog many different obedience training exercises, but let's start with the basics. Sit, stay, come, and down are all essential commands that can make a difference in your dog's behavior. Teaching your pup these basic commands can be a great foundation for more advanced training later on.

When teaching your dog obedience training, consistency is key. Use the same commands and reward system every time so your pup understands what is expected of them. Also, keep training sessions short and sweet. Dogs have short attention spans, and too much training at once can frustrate you and your furry friend.

Here you'll discover many ways you can teach obedience training. Positive reinforcement is an excellent method for teaching your dog obedience training. Another method for teaching obedience training is using a clicker.

Scent Work

Welcome to the exciting world of scent work! Have you ever seen a dog's nose twitching away furiously, trying to sniff out something interesting? That's their scent work instincts kicking in. Dogs love to use their noses and engage in scent work. Not only is it fun for them, but it's also a great way to keep their minds sharp and stimulated. Not only does it provide mental stimulation, but it also gives your dog a sense of purpose and accomplishment. It taps into their instincts and allows them to use their noses to solve puzzles, find hidden objects, and track scents. This activity can also be a great way to build confidence and strengthen your bond with your furry friend.

Several different activities fall under the category of scent work, such as tracking, trailing, and searching. Tracking involves following a specific scent trail left by a person or an object. Trailing is similar to tracking, but it consists in following a scent trail that is fresher and more recent. Searching involves finding a hidden object or substance based on its scent.

Once you have decided on the type of scent work you want to teach your dog, it's time to start. One way to begin is by creating scent trails for your dog to follow. You can do this by placing treats or a favorite toy along a path or hiding them in various locations around the house or yard. Begin with easy trails and increment the difficulty as your dog can.

Another great way to engage your dog in scent work is by playing hide and seek with their favorite toys or treats. Hide the object in a room or area and encourage your dog to find it using its nose. This game provides mental stimulation and physical exercise as your dog moves around to search for hidden objects.

You can also use scent work to teach your dog new obedience commands. For example, you can teach your dog to "stay" while you hide a treat or toy somewhere in the room. Once you've hidden the object, release your dog and encourage them to use their nose to find it. This exercise helps reinforce the "stay" command and engages your dog's senses.

Finally, when teaching scent work, it's important to be patient and take it slow. Dogs have an incredible sense of smell, but developing their skills takes time and practice. Celebrate your dog's successes and encourage them along the way. With consistent practice and positive reinforcement, your dog can become a master sniffer quickly!

Those mental exercises were quite the workout for your pup's brain! But now that they're feeling sharp and focused, it's time to move on to the fun stuff: games! Playing games with your dog is a great way to bond with them and keep them entertained. No matter what you're playing, games can help your pup burn off some energy and have a blast at the same time. So, grab your favorite toy and get ready to play because the next part of this book is all about the best games to play with your furry friend!

Part 🐾5

Let the Games Begin!

A Guide to fun and Interactive Games for Your Dog

Get ready to unleash some serious fun with your furry friend because, in this part, we'll dive into the world of games for your pup. From search games to scent games, we'll cover all the bases to keep your dog engaged, stimulated, and entertained. And don't worry. We won't leave out the foodies - we've got plenty of games that will tantalize your pup's taste buds while also challenging their minds. So put on your game face, grab some treats, and get ready to rumble - it's time to let the games begin!

Search Games

As pet owners, we all know the importance of providing our dogs with regular exercise and playtime. However, did you realize the extent to which mental activity is as relevant to our furry friends as physical exercise? Each dog needs mental stimulation to maintain his brain healthy and sharp. This is where search games come in handy!

You can stimulate your dog's mind and offer him a fun activity through search games. These games can range from simple hide-and-seek games to more complex scent-based games. Search games provide mental stimulation for your dog and encourage them to use their instincts and senses, which is great for their overall health and well-being.

In this chapter, we will explore the world of search games for dogs and provide you with some fun and engaging games to play with your furry friend. I will also provide some tips and tricks for getting started and ensuring that your dog has a safe and enjoyable experience.

Understanding Your Dog's Senses

Before we dive into the exciting world of search games, it's essential to understand your dog's senses. Your furry friend has an extraordinary sense of smell, and it's his primary sense used in search games. They have up to 300 million olfactory receptors, compared to a human's mere 6 million! No wonder they can sniff out a treat from a mile away.

Dogs use their sense of smell to navigate the world around them, and it's essential to stimulate this sense regularly. Search games provide an excellent opportunity to do just that. By hiding treats and toys for your dog to find, you're engaging their sense of smell and keeping their minds active and engaged.

However, it's not just about their sense of smell in search games. Dogs also use their hearing, sight, and touch to locate hidden treasures. It's essential to keep this in mind when designing your search games. You don't want to rely solely on one sense or make it too easy for your pup.

Observing your dog's behavior is critical to understanding their senses and how they use them in search games. You'll want to watch for signs of excitement, such as tail wagging, pawing at the ground, and vocalizations. These signs indicate that your dog uses their senses to search for the hidden object.

You might know that not all dogs have equivalent sensitivity in their senses. For example, some breeds, such as hounds, have a more refined sense of smell than others. Therefore, it's crucial to adjust the difficulty level of the search games accordingly.

Basic Search Game Techniques

These games tap into your dog's instincts, making them feel fulfilled and happy. Let's start with the basics of search games. Trust me, the following techniques that will be outlined are easy to master. With some patience, time, and a few treats, you and your dog will be searched game pros in no time!

Let's introduce some basic search games. These games are ideal for beginners but can also be challenging for more experienced dogs. They are designed to teach your dog the fundamentals of search games while keeping them engaged and having fun.

It would be best if you created the right environment to inspire your dog to use its instincts to search for objects. You can do this by choosing a room or space in your home that is clear of clutter and distractions. Ensure that the objects you use are safe for your dog to handle and interesting enough to keep your dog engaged.

Now it's time to train your dog! The first step is to teach them the "find" command. Start by holding the object in your hand and placing it on the ground before your dog. As they sniff and investigate, say the command "find" and reward them with a treat. Repeat this step until your dog associates the "find" command with the object.

Once your dog has mastered the "find" command, you can begin to hide the object in a more challenging location. Start by hiding it in plain sight and gradually increase the difficulty by hiding it under a blanket or behind a piece of furniture. Praise your furry friend and give him treats when he finds the object.

Keep the game fresh and attractive for your dog. Do this by switching up the objects you use and the locations you hide them in. You can also try playing search games outdoors or incorporate obstacles like boxes or cones to make the game more challenging.

Advanced Search Game Techniques

When it comes to search games, the possibilities are endless. With advanced techniques, you can create even more engaging and challenging games for your dog. These games are perfect for dogs who have mastered basic search games and are looking for more stimulation.

One way to make search games more advanced is using multiple objects and scents. You can create a game where your dog has to search for two or more things hidden in the same area. This will challenge your dog's ability to differentiate between scents and find specific objects. To start, choose a few objects with distinct scents, such as a toy, treat, or piece of clothing. Hide the things in the same area and let your dog sniff them before starting the game. Once your dog is familiar with the scents, ask them to find each object one by one. You can gradually increase the difficulty by hiding the objects in more challenging spots.

Another way to make search games more advanced is by adding time and distance challenges. This will test your dog's ability to search for objects quickly and efficiently. To start, choose a small area to hide an object and time how long it takes your dog to find it. Then, gradually increase the distance between your dog and the thing and see how long it takes them to find it. You can also add a time limit and see how many objects your dog can find within a certain amount of time.

Specialized Search Games

In the previous sections, we covered the basics of search games, techniques to train your dog, and advanced search games. Now, we will delve into specialized search games that challenge your dog's scent discrimination and tracking abilities.

As we know, dogs have an incredible sense of smell, and some breeds, like bloodhounds, have been specifically bred for tracking scents. Specialized search games harness these natural abilities and challenge dogs to identify and differentiate between different scents.

Scent discrimination games involve training your dog to identify specific scents and ignore others. These games can be used for a variety of purposes, from teaching your dog to identify its belongings to detecting specific odors in search and rescue operations.

To do this, you must choose a scent for your dog to focus on. This can be anything from a specific essential oil to a piece of clothing. Begin by presenting the scent to your dog and rewarding them for showing interest in it. Gradually introduce distractions and reward your dog for only focusing on the designated scent.

Tracking games are perfect for dogs who love to explore and follow scents. These games involve training your dog to follow a specific scent trail to find a hidden object or person. This can be a great way to keep your dog mentally stimulated while also getting some exercise. To set up a tracking game, you must create a scent trail by walking with the designated scent in your pocket and leaving small drops along the way. Once you have created the trail, allow your dog to sniff the starting point and encourage them to follow the scent. As they progress, reward them with treats and praise.

Safety and Health Considerations

We all know how important it is to keep our furry friends safe and healthy while playing, and search games are no exception. Since search games can involve hiding objects or treats in unexpected places, it's even more important to take precautions to keep your pup in tip-top shape. So, let's talk about safety and health considerations when searching for games for dogs.

Ensure you supervise your dog during the game, especially if they tend to get over-excited or can be a bit destructive when searching. You don't want your dog to accidentally swallow something they shouldn't or hurt themselves in the process of finding their treasure.

Secondly, always use dog-safe materials for your search games. Avoid using toxic substances, sharp objects, or anything your dog could choke on. It's also a good idea to use toys designed for interactive play to withstand the rough and tumble of search games.

Now, let's talk about some common health concerns to remember when playing search games with your pup. Dehydration is the worst risk, especially if your dog plays outside on a hot day. Ensure your dog can drink fresh water before, during, and after the game. You can also consider using a hydration supplement or adding water to your dog's food to keep them hydrated.

Another concern is over-exertion. While search games are a great way to exercise your dog, it's important not to overdo it. Suspend all games if your dog seems tired or is panting considerably. You can also consider breaking up the game into smaller sessions throughout the day rather than playing for an extended period.

Woof woof, did someone say hunting games for dogs? Time to unleash your dog's wild side in the next chapter!

Hunting Games

Hunting games are a fantastic way to engage your dog's instincts and provide a fun and exciting activity to stimulate them mentally and physically. Whether your dog is a natural-born hunter or just needs a bit of practice, these games will surely bring out the best in them.

You may be thinking, "My dog's not a hunter. They're just couch potatoes!" But fear not! Even the most domesticated dogs have a primal urge to hunt. Hunting games tap into this instinct and allow them to express it in a safe and controlled environment.

This chapter will explore different hunting games you can play with your pup. We'll cover everything from basic hide-and-seek games to more advanced scent-tracking games. By the end of this chapter, your dog will be a pro at hunting games, and you'll have a new favorite activity to bond over.

Understanding Your Dog's Natural Instincts

Let's dive into the exciting world of hunting games for dogs! But before we get started, it's important to understand your furry friend's instincts. Dogs are descendants of wolves and have been bred for centuries to have certain hunting instincts. These instincts include a strong prey drive, excellent tracking skills, and the ability to sniff out even the faintest scents.

Certain dog breeds such as hounds, retrievers, and pointers have been specifically bred for hunting. These breeds possess traits that make them natural-born hunters, such as keen senses, agility, and intelligence.

But even if your pup isn't a breed known for hunting, they still have these instincts buried deep within them. That's why it's important to understand your dog's behavior and observe its natural tendencies. Do they like to sniff out scents on walks? Do they chase after squirrels in the backyard? These can all be signs of your dog's natural hunting instincts.

So, take a step back and observe your dog's behavior. Understanding their instincts will help you better train them and create a fun and safe environment for them to participate in hunting games.

Basic Hunting Game Techniques

To explore the world of basic hunting game techniques for dogs, you need to set up the perfect hunting game environment. You'll want to find a safe and secure location for your pup to practice their hunting skills. This could be a wooded area, a field, or even your backyard (as long as it's fenced in).

Next, it's time to get your furry mate ready for the hunt. Basic obedience training ensures they listen and respond to your commands. Once they've got the basics down, you can start introducing them to hunting-specific commands like "find it" and "fetch."

Now, let's dive into some step-by-step instructions for training your dog in basic hunting games. One of the most common hunting games for dogs is fetch. Follow these steps to coach your dog through this skill:

- Step 1: Choose which game you want to play with your dog. You can use stuffed animals or even actual feathers to make it more authentic. Some popular options include "fetch the duck," "fetch the pheasant," or "fetch the quail."

- Step 2: Get your dog excited about the game by using a high-pitched voice and making lots of noise. Wave the toy around to draw their attention.

- Step 3: Teach your dog the basics of fetching. At first, he throws his toy a small distance, encouraging him to retrieve it. Use lots of praise and treats when they bring it back to you.

- Step 4: Once your dog has the hang of basic fetching, add some obstacles to make it more challenging. For example, you can throw the toy over a small fence or have them retrieve it from under a chair.

- Step 5: Introduce the scent of the game. Rub the toy with the scent of the animal you want him to retrieve and then throw it. Encourage him to use their nose to locate the toy.

- Step 6: Then, gradually increase the distance of your throws, as your furry friend can. This will help to improve their stamina and accuracy.

- Step 7: Finally, it's time to assemble everything and play your chosen hunting game. Use the obstacles and scent to make it more challenging and rewarding for your dog.

Now, let's talk about training your pup to "find it." This game is all about teaching your dog to use its sense of smell to locate a hidden object or treat.

- Step 1: Start with a favorite toy or treat your dog is familiar with. Show it to them, let them sniff it, and then place it in a visible spot for them to retrieve. Once they have retrieved it a few times, hide it in an easy-to-find location while still allowing your dog to see where it is. Then, encourage them to "find it!"

- Step 2: Once your dog has mastered the art of finding the object in an easy-to-find location, start to hide it in more challenging places. Try hiding it behind furniture, under blankets, or in a different room. Make sure to reward your dog with praise and treats when they successfully locate the hidden object.

- <u>Step 3</u>: As your dog gets better at finding the object, you can start to hide it in more difficult spots. For example, you could hide it outside or in a place with distractions like other toys or treats. You can even make a game out of it by timing how long it takes your dog to find the object and trying to beat your best time!
- <u>Step 4</u>: Once your dog has mastered the art of finding objects, you can start to incorporate more things into the game. Try hiding multiple toys or treats in different locations and encourage your dog to find them all.
- <u>Step 5</u>: If your dog is getting the hang of the game, you can start to add a little competition by hiding objects for multiple dogs and seeing who can find their object first.

Remember, the key to successful hunting game training is to keep it fun and engaging for your pup. Reward them with treats and praise when they complete a task. And always keep safety in mind by always supervising your dog and avoiding any potentially dangerous obstacles or areas.

Advanced Hunting Game Techniques

As your furry friend gets more experienced, they'll need new challenges to keep them engaged and excited. So don't be afraid to mix things up! Introduce new types of prey or terrain, incorporating time and distance challenges to keep your dog on its paws.

Another advanced technique is to train your dog to work in teams. Hunting with a partner can be a great bonding experience for your furry friend and can make the hunt more efficient. Dogs must be well-matched in energy level, temperament, and size.

Now, let's talk about different types of prey. As your dog's hunting skills develop, you can introduce them to different types of prey, such as birds, rabbits, or even larger game like deer. Just follow local hunting regulations and never let your dog chase or harm protected wildlife.

Different terrains can also pose new challenges for your dog. Wooded areas may require more scent tracking, while open fields require more speed and agility. By incorporating different terrains into your hunting game, you can keep your dog mentally stimulated and physically fit.

Lastly, let's talk about timing and distance challenges. Try hiding the prey farther away or setting a time limit for your dog to find it. These challenges will help your furry friend build up their stamina and make the hunt more exciting.

Specialized Hunting Games

Plenty of thrilling hunting games will take your furry friend's hunting skills to the next level, such as waterfowl games. If your pup loves to swim, this is the game for them! Waterfowl hunting involves retrieving birds hunted in or near water bodies like lakes, rivers, and marshes. These games require specialized training and skillset, so you must ensure your dog is up for it.

Next up, we have upland bird hunting games. These games are about hunting birds found on the ground, like quails and pheasants. Upland bird hunting games require a lot of focus, agility, and patience from you and your dog. Your furry friend needs to be trained to stay close to you and follow your commands so that they can flush out the birds for you to take down.

To prepare your dog for specialized hunting games, you must ensure that they have had basic training and are well-versed in the rules of hunting games. You can start with basic hunting games and gradually increase the difficulty level until they're ready to take on specialized hunting games.

Hunting Gear and Equipment

For a dog, there's nothing quite like the thrill of the hunt! The great outdoors with fresh air, open fields, and the scent of adventure in the wind. If your pup is a natural-born hunter, having the right gear to keep them safe and comfortable while tracking down their prey is important.

First up, let's talk about collars and leashes. Choose durable hunting collars that can withstand challenging terrain and severe weather conditions. Many hunting dogs wear GPS collars, allowing their owners to track their movements and monitor their safety. For leashes, a long lead is typically best for hunting games, so your dog has plenty of freedom to explore and follow their instincts.

Next, let's talk about hunting clothing and boots. Just like humans, dogs need protection from the elements. A hunting vest or jacket can help keep your pup warm and dry when it's cold outside. And if you're hunting in rough terrain, a good set of boots can protect your dog's paws from sharp rocks and thorns.

Not all hunting gear is created equal. Always make sure you're using gear specifically designed for hunting dogs, as regular pet gear may not be sturdy enough to hold up to the rigors of the hunt.

Safety and Health Considerations

Hunting games are fun activities that can bring out the instincts of our furry friends. However, just like any other activity, we need to take some precautions to ensure the safety and health of our dogs.

Firstly, let's talk about safety. Hunting games often involve guns and other sharp objects, so it's important to always keep your dog on a leash and under your watchful eye. This is especially important if you're hunting in an area where other hunters may be present. Would you like your furry friend accidentally run into danger?

Investing in a high-visibility vest for your dog is also a good idea, especially if you're hunting in an area where there may be other hunters or wildlife. This will help ensure your dog is easily visible and not accidentally mistaken for prey.

Now, let's talk about health considerations. Hunting games can be physically demanding for dogs, so it's essential to ensure your dog is in good physical condition before embarking on a hunt. You should also be aware of the signs of dehydration and heat stroke and take steps to prevent these conditions from occurring.

Investing in some protective gear for your dog, such as booties to protect their paws from sharp objects and cold temperatures is also a good idea. Additionally, you may want to consider a first aid kit specifically designed for dogs, so you're prepared for any injuries that may occur while hunting.

From sniffing out hidden treasures to tracking prey, our furry friends have a knack for exploration and movement. But what happens when they're not out in the wild? That's where movement games come in! These games keep your dog's body and mind active. So, let's put those tails to wag and jump right into the fun next!

Movement Games

Get your dog's paws moving with some exciting movement games for dogs! These games will keep your pup physically fit and provide a mental workout by challenging their problem-solving skills and stimulating their senses. It's a win-win situation that results in a healthier and happier dog.

In this chapter, we'll explore the numerous benefits of movement games, including improved flexibility, increased endurance, and enhanced cognitive abilities. And the best part? You get to bond with your pup while having a blast together!

We'll also dive into various movement games that cater to every dog's needs, from easy-peasy exercises to more advanced activities that will test your pup's skills. So, what are you waiting for? Let's get those tails wagging and get moving!

Getting to Know Your Dog's Innate Behaviors and Tendencies

Dogs love to move and play. It's in their DNA! They use their senses to explore and engage with their environment. You'll know that some dog breeds need activities and exercises to keep them healthy.

Speaking of breeds, certain ones have a higher need for exercise than others. Breeds like Border Collies, Australian Shepherds, and Siberian Huskies were bred to work and require plenty of physical activity to stay healthy. On the other hand, breeds like Bulldogs and Pugs are more laid-back and prefer a more relaxed lifestyle. It's important to consider your dog's breed when planning movement games to ensure they're getting enough exercise for their specific needs.

As I keep saying, every dog is unique and has a personality and habits. By observing your dog's behavior, you can better understand what they enjoy and what their limitations may be. For example, if your dog loves to jump and run, they may enjoy games like agility or frisbee. However, if they have joint issues, they may not be able to handle high-impact activities and may prefer low-impact games like swimming or hiking.

Remember to consider your dog's age, weight, and overall health when planning movement games. It is best to ask your veterinarian before any new activities to ensure your dog is healthy enough for them.

Basic Movement Game Techniques

From classic games like fetch and tug-of-war to newer games like hide-and-seek and agility courses, there's no shortage of ways to get your dog moving. But before we get too carried away, let's ensure we set up a safe environment for our four-legged friends. Whether you're playing in your backyard or at the park, it's essential to ensure there are no hazards around that could cause harm to your pup. This includes things like sharp objects, toxic substances, and areas with high traffic.

Once you've found a safe place to play, it's time to start training your dog. Depending on your pup's age and fitness level, you may need to start with some basic exercises to warm them up. This could include short walks or gentle stretching to prevent injuries.

Once your pup is ready to go, you can start introducing them to some fun movement games. For example, if you're playing fetch, begin with short distances and work up as your dog gets more comfortable. With tug-of-war, make sure to teach your dog to release the toy on command to prevent any accidents.

And don't forget to mix things up to keep your pup engaged and interested! Try playing different games each time you go out to play or switch up the environment to keep things fresh. You can even involve other dogs or friends to make the game more exciting.

More Complex Movement Game Techniques

You've already tackled the basic techniques, so it's time to step up your game and add some new challenges to your pup's exercise routine. You can incorporate obstacles into your movement games. This could include things like jumps, tunnels, and weave poles. Not only will these obstacles challenge your dog's physical abilities, but they'll also help improve their coordination and focus. For example, you could set up a simple agility course using cones, jumps, and tunnels. Start by leading your dog through the course on a leash to show them the route, then gradually remove the leash and encourage them to complete the course on their own.

Next, let's up the ante with time and distance challenges. For instance, you could set up a circuit of stations for your dog to complete, with each station requiring a different movement or action. Time them as they complete the circuit and try to beat their previous record each time.

Another fun challenge is to set up a scavenger hunt for your dog. Hide treats or toys around your home or yard and encourage your dog to find them using their sense of smell and movement. This will not only provide a good workout, but it will also engage their problem-solving skills.

Remember to mix things up so that your dog guesses. Try adding unexpected twists and turns to your movement games or incorporate new toys and objects to keep them interested and engaged.

Specialized Movement Games

Agility training games fall into this category. If you remember, this is where your dog can show off their skills as they race through an obstacle course, weaving through poles, jumping over hurdles, and running through tunnels. It's like a mini doggy Olympics! This type of game is perfect for dogs with a lot of energy and love to run and jump around. Plus, it's a great way to improve your dog's coordination and focus.

There are also flyball games. If your dog is a ball-obsessed maniac, then this is the game for them! In flyball, dogs race against each other in teams, jumping over hurdles to retrieve a tennis ball from a box and bring it back to their handler. It's like a relay race for dogs! This game is great for building your dog's speed and agility and a fantastic way to socialize your pup with other dogs and people.

I bet you're eager to get your furry friend moving and grooving with some fun movement games, but before you get started, it's important to ensure you have the right equipment to keep your dog safe and engaged. You don't need much equipment for simple movement games like fetch or tug-of-war. A sturdy ball or rope toy is usually all you need to get your pup running and jumping around. Of course, it's always a good idea to ensure the toys are durable enough to withstand roughhousing.

Now, if you're ready to step up your game and try more advanced movement activities, you might want to invest in agility equipment like tunnels, jumps, weave poles, and more. The great thing about agility equipment is that it can be customized to fit your dog's size and skill level.

It looks like we've had a good run around with our movement games, but now it's time to chow down and switch gears to some food games in the next chapter. Don't worry. Your pup will still be getting plenty of exercise and stimulation, just with a side of delicious treats.

Food Games

Are you tired of your furry friend always begging for food while you're trying to eat your meal? Have no fear because food games for dogs are here to save the day! In this chapter, we'll explore the wonderful world of food games and their many benefits to your pup's life. Not only do these games provide mental stimulation and entertainment, but they can also improve your dog's overall behavior and health.

We'll cover a variety of food games that you can try with your dog, from simple puzzles to more advanced challenges. And the best part? These games can be played anywhere and anytime, making them a convenient and fun way to engage your dog. So, grab some treats and get ready to have fun with your furry best friend!

Understanding Your Dog's Relationship with Food

Ah, food – the universal language of love. Our furry friends are no exception regarding their love of all things delicious. But did you know that food games can do more than just satisfy your dog's appetite? That's right. Food games can also be used to improve your dog's mental and physical well-being.

First, let's take a look at a dog's relationship with food. Dogs are natural scavengers, always on the hunt for their next meal. In the wild, they would have to search for food and compete with other animals. This means that they have a strong drive to seek out and consume food.

But in our modern world, food is often readily available and easily accessible. This can lead to dogs overeating or becoming picky eaters. Understanding your dog's instincts and behaviors around food can help you create a healthy relationship with food and avoid any negative consequences.

When it comes to eating habits, dogs can be quite varied. Some dogs are notorious for scarfing down their food in record time, while others take their time to savor every bite. Some dogs are picky eaters and will only eat certain types of food, while others will eat anything and everything. Observe your dog's eating habits and behaviors to ensure they're healthy and happy. Is your dog eating too quickly? This could lead to digestive issues or choking. Is your dog not eating at all? This could be a sign of a health issue. By paying attention to their eating habits, you can ensure they get the nutrition they need.

Now that we understand our dog's relationship with food let's explore how food games can benefit them.

Food Game Techniques

When it comes to the types of food games you can play with your dog, the possibilities are endless! Simple games like hide-and-seek or scavenger hunts can be great for beginners. For hide-and-seek, simply hide small treats around the room and encourage your pup to search for them using their nose. Scavenger hunts involve hiding food or treats in various locations throughout the house or yard and giving your dog clues to find them.

Another basic food game is the classic "food puzzle" toy. These toys are designed to hold food or treats and require your dog to figure out how to access them. They can be found in a variety of shapes and sizes, from simple puzzle balls to more complex maze-like toys.

Lastly, we have the "memory game." This is where you show your pup a treat, then hide it under one of three cups. Shuffle the cups around and see if your puppy can remember which cup the treat is under. Start with one cup and work your way up to more cups as your pup gets better. You can also incorporate different types of food and difficulty levels. You can use a variety of foods for these games, including kibble, canned food, fruits, and vegetables. Switching up the type of food will keep your pup interested and excited to play. You can adjust the difficulty level by changing the hiding spots or making the puzzle toys harder to solve.

Also, you can set a timer for your pup to see how quickly they can complete the food game. This will add a bit of friendly competition and encourage your puppy to work quickly. You can also increase the distance between your pup and the food to make the game more challenging. This will require your pup to use their nose and problem-solving skills even more.

Equipment for Food Games

Up next for discussion is the essential equipment for food games. These include food-dispensing toys, which come in a variety of shapes and sizes. There are puzzle toys that require your dog to figure out how to get to the food, and then there are treat balls that dispense food as your dog rolls them around.

Puzzle toys are perfect for dogs who like a challenge. These toys typically have hidden compartments or tricky mechanisms that require some brain power to figure out. They can be a great way to keep your dog's mind active and engaged. Treat balls, on the other hand, are great for dogs who love to play and be active. Simply fill them with food; your dog can roll and chase them around for hours.

Don't forget to consider your dog's size, age, and activity level when selecting food-dispensing toys.

Safety and Health Considerations

Just like with any activity involving your dog, safety should always be a top priority. Regarding food games, it's essential to ensure your dog isn't consuming too much food too quickly, which can lead to choking or other health issues. It's also important to supervise your dog during food games to ensure they aren't getting into unsafe situations or potentially harmful items.

While food games can be a great way to provide mental stimulation and exercise for your dog, ensure you are aware of any underlying health issues that may affect their ability to participate. For example, if your dog has dental issues, certain types of food or toys may not be suitable for them.

You can do several things to ensure that your dog stays safe and healthy while enjoying their food games. First, make sure to choose high-quality, nutritious food appropriate for your dog's age and size. This can help prevent any digestive issues that may arise from consuming low-quality or inappropriate foods. It's also essential to choose food-dispensing toys that are the appropriate size for your dog to prevent any choking hazards.

Another way to protect your dog is to supervise them while they play food games. This can help ensure they aren't consuming too much food too quickly or getting into potentially harmful situations. Additionally, you can use slow feeders or puzzles to help slow down your dog's eating and provide a more mentally stimulating activity.

Hold onto your leashes! We're about to dive into a new chapter on dog games, and this time we're getting wet! That's right. We're talking about diving and water games next!

Diving And Water Games

Get ready to make a splash with your furry friend with the exciting world of diving and water games for dogs! These games are a fun way to cool off during the hot summer months and provide numerous health benefits for your canine companion.

This chapter will explore the many benefits of water games for dogs, including improved cardiovascular health, muscle strength, and overall well-being. We'll also dive into the different types of water games you can try with your dog, from basic swimming to advanced diving techniques.

So, grab your life jacket, sunscreen, and your furry best friend, and let's dive into the world of water games for dogs!

What Are Your Dog's Natural Instincts in the Water?

The water is a place of refreshment, relaxation, and fun - at least for humans. But what about our furry friends? Do they share the same enthusiasm for the water, or are they more like cats, utterly uninterested in taking a dip? Well, the answer is not so black and white. Some dogs are born water babies, while others prefer to stay on dry land. So, let's dive in (pun intended) and explore your dog's instincts in the water!

First, not all dogs are created equal when it comes to swimming. Some breeds were born to swim, while others are more suited for other activities, like fetching or lounging around. For example, Retrievers, Newfoundlands, and Portuguese Water Dogs are some of the most water-loving breeds out there. They have webbed feet, thick coats, and strong swimming skills, making them excellent aquatic athletes. On the other hand, breeds like Pugs, Bulldogs, and Basset Hounds are not exactly built for the water. They have short snouts, heavy bodies, and a low center of gravity, making it challenging for them to stay afloat.

But regardless of breed, all dogs have an innate sense of curiosity and exploration. When it comes to the water, some may be hesitant initially, while others will jump right in without a second thought. As a responsible pet owner, observing your dog's behavior in and around water is essential to ensure their safety. If your dog shows signs of anxiety or discomfort, gradually introducing them to the water is best.

One of the best ways to encourage your dog's instincts in the water is through play. Dogs love to fetch, and what's better than playing fetch in the water? It's a win-win situation: your dog gets to exercise their swimming skills, and you get to cool off on a hot day. Just use a waterproof toy, like a floating ball or Frisbee, to avoid accidents or injuries.

In addition, to fetch, you can play other water games with your dog to enhance their swimming abilities. For example, you can create a simple obstacle course in the water using pool noodles, hula hoops, or other buoyant objects. You can also try teaching your dog how to dive for toys, which strengthens their swimming skills and problem-solving abilities.

Basic Water Game Techniques

Whether your furry companion is a natural-born swimmer or just dipping their paws into the water, water games can be a great way to keep them active, cool them down on hot days, and strengthen your bond with them. So, let's set sail and explore the basics of water games for dogs!

Before you get your dog into the water, ensure the environment is safe. Depending on where you're playing, you may need to consider factors such as water depth, currents, and obstacles. If you're playing in a pool, ensure your dog knows where the steps or ladder are, so they can easily exit the pool if they tire. Investing in a dog life jacket is also a good idea, especially for dogs that are new to swimming or have difficulty staying afloat.

Once you've ensured the environment's safety, introduce your dog to the water. Start by letting your dog explore the water on his terms, either by letting him wade in shallow water or by using a ramp or shallow steps to ease him into the deeper water.

When your dog is ready, you can start introducing some basic water games. These can include games like fetch or chase, using a floating toy or ball. Start by throwing the toy or ball a short distance and encouraging your dog to swim out and retrieve it. As your dog gets more comfortable in the water, you can gradually increase the distance and difficulty of the game.

Watch for signs of fatigue, such as slowing down, shaking or shivering, or difficulty staying afloat. If your dog seems tired or uncomfortable, it's essential to take a break and let them rest.

Advanced Water Game Techniques

So, do you think your furry first mate is ready to take their aquatic adventures to the next level? Well, shiver me timbers. I've got just the thing for you! Let's talk about advanced water game techniques for your pup.

Firstly, let's talk about incorporating obstacles and challenges. Just like with land-based agility courses, setting up a course in the water can provide a fun and challenging way to engage your dog. You can use buoys, pool noodles, or floating toys to create a course that your pup must swim through, around, or under. You can also add jumps, where your dog has to jump over an obstacle in the water, such as a floating hoop.

Another advanced technique is adding time and distance challenges. This can include having your dog retrieve a toy from a further distance or timing how long it takes to swim from one end of the pool to the other. To make it even more challenging, you can add distractions such as throwing a ball for another dog nearby or having someone else swim in the pool.

Specialized Water Games

We've got some exciting games to share that will make your dog the captain of the water world. First up, we have dock diving games. This fun game involves your dog jumping off a dock into the water and retrieving a toy or object. The game is all about distance, height, and accuracy. Your dog must be a good swimmer and should love to retrieve things from the water.

To get started, you'll need to find a safe dock for your dog to jump off. You can also use a platform or a pool if you don't have access to a dock. Next, you'll need a toy or object your dog loves to retrieve. This could be a ball, a frisbee, or a buoy.

Once you have everything set up, toss the toy into the water and encourage your dog to jump in and retrieve it. Gradually increase the distance of the toss and work on accuracy by placing the toy in different areas of the water. You can also work on height by placing the toy on a higher surface and encouraging your dog to jump and retrieve it.

Next, we have retrieval games. This game involves your dog swimming out to retrieve and bring an object back to you. The game can be played with various things, such as balls, sticks, or toys. The game is all about speed, accuracy, and distance. To participate in this game, find a safe area with calm water and toss the object a short distance away. Encourage your dog to swim out and retrieve the object, and then bring it back to you. Gradually increase the distance of the toss and work on accuracy by placing the thing in different areas of the water. You can also work on speed by timing how long your dog takes to retrieve and bring the object back to you.

Gear for Water Games

We need to make sure that your pup stays safe in the water. Depending on your dog's swimming abilities, you may want to invest in a life jacket. Not all dogs are natural swimmers, and even if your pup is, the extra buoyancy provided by a life jacket can be a lifesaver in rough waters. Look for an adjustable jacket with a handle on top for easy lifting and brightly colored for visibility.

Next, let's talk about toys. Many water toys are available for dogs, but some are better suited for specific activities. For example, a frisbee may be great for playing fetch on land, but it's not very buoyant and can be difficult for your dog to retrieve in the water. Look for toys designed for water play, like floating balls or toys with rope handles that make it easier for your dog to retrieve them. Some toys even dispense treats or have spaces for you to add food, making water games even more exciting for your furry friend.

Lastly, don't forget to protect your pup's eyes and ears. Chlorine, saltwater, and other irritants can cause discomfort or even infection. Goggles or a mask can help protect your dog's eyes, while earplugs can prevent water from getting into their ears.

When choosing gear for your dog's water games, cater to your dog's size, swimming abilities, and personal preferences. Some dogs may prefer toys that are easy to grip or float low in the water, while others may enjoy the challenge of retrieving toys that are farther away or require diving.

Safety and Health Considerations

Just like with any activity, there are risks involved with water games. Dogs can quickly become tired or overwhelmed in the water, especially if they're not experienced swimmers. It's important always to supervise your dog while in the water and never leave them unattended. You never know when a sneaky wave might come along and sweep your pup out to sea.

In addition to supervision, it's essential to be aware of any potential hazards in the water. Sharp rocks, strong currents, and dangerous wildlife are just a few things to watch. Ensure the area where you're playing with your dog is safe and free from potential dangers.

It's also important to make sure your dog is up to date on their vaccinations and parasite preventatives. Water is a common breeding ground for parasites like ticks and fleas, so make sure your dog is protected before taking them for a swim. Additionally, if you're playing in a natural body of water, be aware of the risk of waterborne illnesses like leptospirosis.

Last but not least, don't forget to take some preventative measures to protect your dog. Ensure they can access fresh water to prevent dehydration and take breaks if your dog seems tired. If you're playing in the sun, ensure your dog has access to shade to avoid overheating. And always rinse your dog off with fresh water after playing in the saltwater, as salt can dry and irritate their skin.

As your furry companion dries off after a thrilling water game session, it's time to move on to some activities that will challenge their minds. Dogs are intelligent creatures, and it's important to keep their brains and bodies engaged. In the coming chapter, let's dive into the world of intelligence games for dogs!

Intelligence Games

Did you know that the average dog has the intelligence level of a 2-year-old human? That's right. Your pup is pretty smart! However, just like people, each dog has unique strengths and weaknesses regarding intelligence. Some may excel at problem-solving, while others may be better at social intelligence. That's why it's important to observe and understand your dog's intelligence level and cater to their specific needs when playing intelligence games. Let's challenge those furry brains and dive into the world of intelligence games for dogs in this chapter!

Intelligence Game Techniques

If your dog is chewing on everything in sight or constantly begging for your attention, then it might be time to give their brain a workout with some basic intelligence games. Intelligence games are a fun and interactive way to stimulate your dog's mind and improve their problem-solving skills. You don't even need a lot of fancy equipment to get started.

To begin, set up a safe and stimulating game environment. This can be as simple as clearing a space in your living room or backyard or creating an obstacle course using household items like chairs and boxes.

Next, you'll want to choose a game that suits your dog's personality and skill level. For example, if your dog loves to sniff and explore, a game of hide-and-seek with treats or toys could be perfect. Or if they enjoy using their paws and nose, a game of shell game or treat cups could be a hit.

Once you've selected a game, begin training your dog. Start with simple commands, such as "sit" and "stay," and gradually introduce the game mechanics. Be patient and encouraging and remember to reward your dog with plenty of praise and treats when they succeed.

Are you ready to level up your dog's intelligence game? We're talking about taking your puppy from basic obedience to canine genius! One technique to try is increasing the level of difficulty and complexity in the game. Another method is incorporating time and distance challenges.

It's important to remember that not all dogs learn at the same pace or have the same level of interest in every game. So, don't be discouraged if your dog doesn't pick up on a new game right away. Be patient and try different techniques until you find the ones that work best for your pup. Now that we've explored the world of intelligence games, it's time to shift our focus to another aspect of canine well-being: balance. Like humans, dogs benefit from exercises challenging their balance and stability. So, let's dive into the world of balancing games and explore some fun and stimulating ways to keep your furry friend on their paws next!

Balancing Games

It's time we take the phrase "paws for balance" to a new level! This chapter will explore the wonderful world of balance and coordination and how you can help your furry friend develop these skills through fun and engaging games.

Why should you bother with balancing games, you ask? Well, they are a fun way to bond with your dog and provide mental stimulation, and they also have some pretty impressive physical benefits. Just like us humans, dogs need to have good balance and coordination to maintain their posture, walk properly, and avoid injuries.

Furthermore, practicing balance games can help strengthen your dog's core muscles, improve their flexibility, and increase their overall body awareness. These skills are essential for dogs participating in sports, like agility or flyball, or recovering from an injury.

But don't worry. You don't need a fancy gym or equipment to start incorporating balance games into your dog's routine. You can start with everyday household items like cushions, pillows, or even a wobble board if you happen to have one lying around. Plus, you'll get to enjoy watching your dog's comical attempts to stay upright, which is guaranteed to provide some laughs and entertainment.

In this chapter, we'll explore a range of different balancing games, from simple to more advanced levels. We'll cover everything from teaching your dog to stand on a cushion to walking across a balance beam like a pro. We'll also discuss safety considerations, how to choose the right equipment for your dog, and how to ensure that your dog is progressing at a pace that is comfortable for them.

So, get ready to "paws" and take a step into the world of balancing games for dogs. Trust me, you and your dog are in for a treat!

A Dog's Balance

Let's talk about balance, but not the kind you need to pay your bills or keep your social life in check. We're talking about your dog's balance – keeping them on their paws and ready to tackle any challenge.

Like humans, dogs rely on balance to navigate the world around them. From running and playing to jumping and climbing, balance is essential to their physical abilities. Without proper balance, dogs can struggle to perform everyday tasks and may even be at risk for injury.

So, what exactly is balance when it comes to dogs? Well, it's the ability to maintain a stable center of gravity while moving or standing. This involves coordination between their muscles, joints, and nervous system to keep their body alignment.

Factors such as age, weight, and breed can all affect a dog's natural balance. For example, smaller breeds may have an easier time balancing on narrow surfaces, while larger breeds may struggle due to their size and weight.

But regardless of their breed or size, maintaining proper balance is crucial for a dog's overall health and well-being. It can improve their agility, coordination, and even their confidence.

Now that we understand the importance of balance for dogs let's dive deeper into how we can help them develop and maintain their skills through balancing games.

Balance Game Techniques

To take your dog's balance game to the next level, you can incorporate different difficulty and complexity levels. Start by adding obstacles to your dog's balance routine. You can use items such as cones, agility poles, or even household objects like cushions or pillows. Place them in different arrangements and heights to keep your dog guessing and engaged.

Another great way to advance your dog's balance game is to incorporate distance and time challenges. Start by having your dog hold a position on a balance ball or wobble board for some time. Gradually increase the time and add more challenges, like a treat or toy placed just out of reach to keep them engaged and motivated. You can also increase the distance your dog travels across an obstacle course, whether on a balance beam or a series of platforms.

It's important to remember that safety should always come first when it comes to advanced balance games. Ensure your dog is comfortable with the basic techniques before introducing new challenges. Always supervise your dog during training and use safety gear like a harness or safety leash to prevent falls and injuries.

Equipment for Balance Games

To put your pup's balance skills to the test, you'll need the right equipment for the job. Let's start with an overview of the essential equipment for balance games. First and foremost, you'll want to invest in a balance board. Balance boards come in a variety of shapes and sizes, but they all have one thing in common - they challenge your dog's sense of balance by requiring them to maintain stability while standing or walking on an unstable surface.

There are also balance discs, essentially large inflatable cushions that can create an unstable surface for your dog to stand or sit on. These are great for introducing your pup to the concept of balance games, as they are relatively easy to master but still provide a good workout for their core muscles.

Another popular piece of equipment for balance games is the FitPAWS® Donut. This is a large inflatable ring. It can help your dog develop better balance, coordination, and proprioception (awareness of their body in space). The donut can be used as a standalone piece of equipment or with other balance toys.

Of course, there are plenty of other balance toys and props out there that you can use to challenge your dog's balance skills. For example, you could set up a series of cones or agility poles for your dog to weave in and out of while maintaining their balance. Or you could use a balance beam or narrow plank for them to walk across.

When choosing the right equipment for your dog, there are a few things to keep in mind. First, you'll want to consider your dog's size and weight. Ensure that your chosen equipment is appropriate for your dog's size and won't tip over or collapse under their weight.

You'll also want to consider your dog's skill level. If he is new to balancing games, you'll want to start with simpler equipment and work up to more challenging toys and props as he improves. Finally, safety should always be a top priority when choosing equipment for your dog. Make sure that the equipment you choose is sturdy and well-constructed.

Safety and Health Considerations

While balance games can be fun and challenging to engage your dog's body and mind, taking precautions to prevent accidents and injuries is important.

One key safety consideration is ensuring that your dog is properly trained and prepared for the specific balance game you are playing. For example, if you practice a balance beam exercise, your dog should be comfortable walking on a flat surface before attempting the beam. Additionally, you should always supervise your dog during balance games and be ready to intervene if necessary.

It's also essential to keep the environment safe for your dog to play in. Ensure the surface is non-slip and free of any obstacles that could cause tripping or falling. Consider using mats or padding to cushion falls or slips.

It's also important to be mindful of your dog's physical limitations and any pre-existing conditions they may have. Certain balance games, such as those requiring jumping or sudden movements, may not be suitable for dogs with joint issues or other mobility concerns.

Another health consideration is proper warm-up and cool-down exercises. So, picture this: You're lounging on the couch, wrapped up in your favorite blanket, binging your favorite TV show. Suddenly, your friend bursts through the door and drags you off the couch, demanding you sprint a mile with them. You protest, saying you haven't warmed up, but your friend doesn't care and drags you out the door anyway. You start running but quickly realize that your muscles are tight and your body isn't ready for this sudden burst of activity. You end up hobbling back home, sore and regretful.

Well, that's what it's like for your dog if you don't warm them up properly before any workout. Like humans, dogs need to ease into physical activity to prevent injury and strain. Proper warm-up exercises can help to loosen up their muscles and joints, increase their heart rate, and prepare them for more strenuous activity.

And let's not forget about cool-down exercises. After a workout, your dog's body is all fired up, and their heart rate is elevated. If you suddenly stop their activity and send them back to their cozy bed, their muscles can tighten up and become sore. Cool-down exercises can help to gradually bring their heart rate back down and prevent stiffness and soreness.

As can be seen, just like humans, dogs need to prepare their bodies for physical activity gradually and adequately cool down afterward. Take a few minutes to walk or stretch with your dog before and after balance games to help prevent strains or other injuries.

Finally, always provide your dog plenty of fresh water and breaks during playtime to prevent overheating and exhaustion.

Balancing Games for Specific Needs

Did you know these games can also be tailored to dogs with specific needs? That's right - even seniors, dogs with disabilities, and dogs in agility training can benefit from balancing games.

Let's first look at the benefits to senior dogs. As dog's age, their balance and mobility may start to decline, which can lead to a decrease in overall physical health. But balancing games can help improve balance and strengthen muscles, improving overall health. Simple balancing games like "paws up" (where the dog stands with their front paws on an elevated surface) and "cookie stretches" (where the dog reaches for a treat placed just out of reach) can be great for senior dogs.

For dogs with disabilities, balancing games can be a bit more challenging to navigate. However, with some creativity and patience, these pups still have plenty of options. For example, a dog with a missing limb can benefit from balancing games that focus on strengthening their remaining limbs. A dog with vision impairment can benefit from games focusing on sound and touch, such as a game where they have to find treats hidden in different textures.

Finally, balancing games can also be a valuable tool for dogs in agility training. Agility requires a lot of balance and coordination, so practicing balancing games can help prepare a dog for the challenges of an agility course. Games like "balance beam" (where the dog walks across a narrow beam) and "tippy board" (where the dog must balance on an unstable surface) can help improve a dog's agility skills.

Of course, no matter your dog's specific needs, it's always important to keep safety in mind. For senior dogs and dogs with disabilities, make sure that the balancing games are appropriate for their physical abilities and that they are not at risk of injury. For dogs in agility training, start with simpler balancing games and gradually work up to more challenging ones.

I hope you and your furry friend enjoyed working on your balance. Now, let's focus on another important aspect of your dog's well-being - their mental focus! Like humans, dogs need to exercise their brains and stay sharp. In the next chapter, we'll be exploring some exciting focus games that will keep your dog's mind engaged and sharp as a whistle.

focus Games

Dogs are intelligent animals, and they thrive on mental and physical stimulation. Focus games provide both! By playing focus games with your dog, you'll help them improve their concentration and problem-solving skills. Plus, it's fun to bond with your pup and build trust between you two. In this chapter, we'll cover a range of focus games designed to challenge your dog's mind and help them improve their focus. We'll give you step-by-step instructions for each game, so you can easily play them with your pup at home. Plus, we'll provide tips on how to make each game more challenging as your dog improves. So, get ready to have some fun with your furry friend! In the following sections, we'll dive into the world of focus games and give you all the tools you need to help your dog improve their concentration and problem-solving skills.

Focus Game Techniques

Just like humans, dogs can get easily distracted by all the exciting things around them, but that doesn't mean they can't learn how to focus on their humans. Playing focus games can help them become more attentive and responsive to their owners, improving their behavior and making them better companions.

When it comes to basic focus game techniques, it's important to start with simple activities to help them understand what's expected. For example, you can hold a treat in front of their nose and slowly move it towards their face, and when they make eye contact with you, reward them with the treat and lots of praise. Repeat this exercise several times a day, gradually increasing the amount of time they need to maintain eye contact before getting the treat.

Once they've mastered the basics, it's time to move on to more challenging focus games. This could include activities such as teaching them to ignore distractions like other dogs or people while walking on a leash or having them follow a target stick or a moving object with their eyes. These games require more concentration and focus, but they can be incredibly rewarding for dogs and their owners.

And for dogs already pros at the basic focus games, the advanced techniques are where the real fun begins. This could include incorporating more complex obstacles, such as weaving through cones or jumping over hurdles, while maintaining focus on our owner. They can also work on more extended time and distance challenges, where they must maintain focus for several minutes or follow commands from a distance.

The key to success with focus games is to make them fun and engaging for the dog. They love nothing more than spending time with their owners and getting lots of praise and treats for doing a good job. So, get creative with your focus games and try to incorporate activities that both you and your dog enjoy. And before you know it, they'll be focused and attentive pups, ready to tackle any challenge that comes our way.

Equipment for Focus Games

Are you ready to take your pup's focus to the next level? Then let's discuss the equipment you'll need to make it happen. First up, we have interactive toys. These can be a great way to engage your dog's brain and help them focus on a task. Look for toys that require your dog to manipulate them to get a reward, such as puzzle toys or treat-dispensing balls.

Next, we have props such as cones, poles, and jumps. These can be used to create an agility-style course for your dog to navigate, helping them focus on following your cues and commands.

Last but not least, consider using a clicker to mark desired behavior and reinforce positive actions. Remember, focus games aim to strengthen your dog's attention and obedience skills while having fun and building your bond. So, choose equipment to help achieve that goal and keep your furry friend engaged and entertained.

Focus Games for Specific Needs

Focus games are like the doggy version of meditation. Instead of sitting still and quiet, your pup is bouncing around, but it's a start! Focus games are a great way to strengthen your pup's attention span and improve their ability to focus on you. And the best part? They can be tailored to suit your dog's specific needs, whether a puppy, a senior, or suffering from anxiety. So, let's dive in!

Puppies have the attention span of a goldfish. That's why it's essential to start them off with simple focus games that are easy to understand. A great game to start with is the "Name Game." This game involves calling your puppy's name and rewarding them with a treat when they look at you. As your puppy gets better at the game, you can increase the difficulty by calling their name from different locations or when distractions are around.

Another game that is perfect for puppies is "Watch Me." This game involves holding a treat in your hand and bringing it to your face while saying, "Watch Me." When your puppy makes eye contact with you, reward them with the treat. As they improve at the game, you can increase the distance between you and your puppy.

As dogs get older, they can start to lose their hearing and vision, making it difficult to focus. An excellent game for senior dogs is "Find It." This game involves hiding treats around the house and encouraging your dog to find them. This game not only helps to improve their focus but also keeps them active and engaged.

Another game that is perfect for senior dogs is "Touch." This game involves teaching your dog to touch your hand with its nose. This game is excellent for improving your dog's focus and strengthening the bond between you and your furry friend.

Dogs that suffer from anxiety can benefit significantly from focus games. A great game for anxious dogs is "Slow Treat." This game involves treating your dog and covering it with your hand. Your dog will need to focus on you to get the treat. This game not only helps to improve your dog's focus but can also help to calm them down.

Another game that is perfect for anxious dogs is "Mat Work." This game involves teaching your dog to go to their mat and lay down. This game can help your dog to feel more comfortable and secure in its space, improving its overall focus and reducing anxiety levels.

We've covered focus games, where we taught our pups to stay attentive, but now it's time to switch gears to something a bit harder - impulse control. Meet me in the next chapter.

Impulse Control Games

Impulse control is something most of us struggle with at some point in our lives. Maybe it's the urge to buy yet another pair of shoes when we have a closet full already or the compulsion to eat that last slice of pizza even though we're already stuffed. Well, guess what? Dogs struggle with impulse control, too!

Take a trip down this visualization trail with me. Picture that you come home after a long day at work, and your dog is ecstatic to see you. Tail wagging, tongue lolling, he bounces around like a trampoline kid. You sit down on the couch to relax, and before you know it, he's leaped onto your lap and is trying to lick your face off. Sure, it's adorable - but it can also be annoying and dangerous if your dog is large or overly enthusiastic.

Enter impulse control training. By teaching your dog to resist his impulses and wait for your signal, you can help him learn to behave appropriately in a variety of situations. Impulse control games are a fun and effective way to teach your dog self-control, patience, and focus.

But why bother with impulse control training in the first place? For one thing, it can help prevent problem behaviors like jumping, pulling on the leash, and counter-surfing. It can also make your dog safer around people and other animals, making him less likely to lunge or react impulsively.

Plus, impulse control training can be enjoyable for your dog! Dogs are intelligent creatures who love learning and playing games with them is a great way to bond and have fun.

So, how do impulse control games work? The science behind it is pretty simple. When it comes to teaching your dog to resist impulses and wait for your signal, you're tapping into a pretty sophisticated aspect of their brain. The prefrontal cortex is responsible for decision-making, self-control, and complex thinking. So, when your dog waits for you to give the command to fetch or go for a walk, they use this highly developed part of their brain.

Now, as you practice impulse control with your dog, you're strengthening the connections in their prefrontal cortex. This is because the more your dog practices waiting for your signal, the stronger the neural pathways in its brain become. With repeated practice, your dog will become better at regulating their behavior and making smarter decisions at the moment.

Of course, every dog is different, and some may take to impulse control training more readily than others. But with patience, consistency, and a healthy dose of humor, you can teach your dog to be the master of his impulses - and maybe even learn a thing or two about impulse control yourself!

So, let's get started with some fun and effective impulse control games for dogs.

Fun Impulse Control Games for Dogs

Have you ever played a game of catch with your dog, only to have him snatch the ball out of your hand before you even have a chance to throw it? Or maybe you've been playing tug-of-war with your pup, and he just won't let go of the toy, no matter how many times you ask him to "drop it." Trust me. We've all been there.

But what if I told you could play fun and effective games with your dog to help him develop impulse control and learn to listen to you? That's right - by teaching your dog to "wait," "drop it," and "catch" on command, you can help him become a better-behaved and more attentive companion. Let's start with "wait." This great impulse control game can be played anywhere, anytime - all you need is your dog and a few treats. Start by asking your dog to sit or lie down, then hold a treat just out of his reach. As soon as he starts to reach for the treat, say, "Wait," and move the treat away. If your dog stays still, give him the treat and lots of praise. If he tries to grab the treat, move it farther away and start again.

Over time, you can gradually increase the amount of time you ask your dog to wait before giving him the treat. This will help him learn to control his impulses and focus on you rather than just trying to grab the treat as quickly as possible.

Next up is "drop it." This is a crucial command for any dog who loves to play with toys, as it can help prevent them from accidentally swallowing or choking on something they shouldn't have. To teach your dog to drop a toy on command, start by playing tug-of-war or fetch with him. When it's time to end the game, hold a treat in front of his nose and say, "Drop it." When he lets go of the toy to take the treat, give him lots of praise and repeat the command. Over time, your dog will learn to associate the command with letting go of the toy, even without the treat.

Finally, there's a "catch." This game can help your dog develop focus, hand-eye coordination, and impulse control. Start by tossing a treat to your dog and saying, "Catch." If he catches the treat, praise him and repeat the command. If he doesn't catch it, no worries - just try again. Over time, you can increase the difficulty by tossing the treat higher or farther away or even bouncing it off a wall.

Impulse Control Training for Specific Issues

If you're a dog owner, you've probably experienced at least one issue with your furry friend's impulse control. These behaviors can be frustrating and even dangerous in some situations, whether it's food aggression, toy possessiveness, jumping on people, or chasing other animals. But don't worry - with some patience and training. You can help your dog develop better impulse control and overcome these issues.

Let's start with food aggression. This is when your dog becomes possessive or aggressive around his food, often growling or even biting if anyone tries to approach. To address this behavior, start by feeding your dog in a separate room or area away from other pets or family members. This will help him feel less territorial about his food. Then, slowly introduce people or other pets into the room while he's eating, gradually increasing the level of distraction over time. If he starts to show signs of aggression, remove the distractions and try again later. With consistent practice, your dog will learn that it's okay to share his food and that he doesn't need to be possessive.

Next up is toy possessiveness. This is when your dog becomes overly protective of his toys, growling or biting if anyone tries to take them away. To address this behavior, teach your dog the "drop it" command (see my previous response!). Then, practice playing with your dog's toys and rewarding him for letting you take them away and giving them back. This will help him learn that sharing his toys is okay and that he doesn't need to be possessive.

Jumping on people is another common impulse control issue. This is when your dog gets excited and jumps up on people, potentially knocking them over or causing injury. To address this behavior, start by teaching your dog the "sit" command and rewarding him for sitting calmly when people approach. Then, practice having people approach and reward him for staying seated. Over time, your dog will learn that sitting is better than jumping up on people.

Finally, there's chasing other animals. This is when your dog becomes overly excited and starts chasing after other animals, potentially putting himself in danger or causing harm to the other animal. To address this behavior, keep your dog on a leash and practice the "leave it" command. When you see another animal, say "leave it" and reward your dog for looking at you instead of trying to chase the other animal. With consistent practice, your dog will learn to control his impulses and focus on you instead of chasing after other animals.

Incorporating Impulse Control into Daily Life

We've talked about impulse control games you can play with your dog, but did you know you can also incorporate impulse control into your daily life with your furry friend? That's right - practicing good impulse control habits can help your dog become a more well-behaved and obedient companion.

One way to do this is using impulse control games in everyday situations. For example, when you're about to take your dog on a walk, ask him to sit and stay before opening the door. This will help him learn to control his impulses and wait for your command before taking action. Another example is using the "wait" command before giving your dog his food or treat. This will help him learn to wait patiently and control his impulses instead of snatching the food out of your hand.

Another way to incorporate impulse control into daily life is by combining it with obedience training. For example, when teaching your dog the "stay" command, you can also teach him to control his impulses by only rewarding him when he stays still and doesn't move. This will help him learn to control his impulses and wait for your command before acting.

Of course, it's essential to maintain good impulse control habits regularly. This means consistently practicing impulse control games and incorporating them into your daily routine. It also means being patient with your dog and not expecting him to be perfect right away. Remember, impulse control is a skill that takes time and practice to develop, just like any other skill.

Now that we've worked on impulse control, it's time to talk about those moments when your pup is left alone at home. Don't worry. We've got some fun and stimulating games for him to play independently! Let's dive into the next chapter.

Games to Play When the Dog Is Left Alone at Home

Being away from your furry friend can be challenging, but it doesn't have to be boring for them. There are plenty of games and activities you can set up for your dog to keep them occupied and happy while you're away. Examples Include puzzle toys. These are toys designed to challenge your dog's problem-solving skills and keep their minds active and engaged. No more getting bored and chewing on the couch!

There are different types of puzzle toys, but the basic idea is to hide treats or kibble inside the toy, and your dog has to figure out how to get to them. Some toys have compartments your dog can slide or lift open, while others have rotating parts or multiple layers.
The best part about puzzle toys is that they come in all shapes and sizes, so you can find one that suits your dog's preferences and skill level. Some are made of hard plastic, while others are made of soft fabric or rubber. Some puzzle toys are even designed for water use, which is excellent for water-loving dogs!
Another great way to keep your dog occupied is through interactive treat dispensers. These toys combine playtime with snack time, making them perfect for dogs who get bored easily or have separation anxiety when their owners are away.

Interactive treat dispensers come in all shapes and sizes, from small puzzle balls to larger, more complex toys. The basic idea is that your dog has to figure out how to get the treats out of the dispenser, which keeps them engaged and mentally stimulated.

There are a few different types of treat dispensers to choose from:

- <u>Puzzle Feeders</u> - These toys have hidden compartments or maze-like structures that require your dog to use problem-solving skills to get to the treats. Some puzzle feeders have multiple difficulty levels, so you can start with an easier one and work your way up as your dog gets better at solving puzzles.
- <u>Wobblers</u> - These toys have a weighted bottom, which means they wobble and move around as your dog plays with them. This movement makes it harder for your dog to get to the treats inside, so they must work harder to figure it out.
- <u>Ball Launchers</u> - These toys are like mini-pinball machines for dogs. You load them up with treats, and then your dog has to figure out how to launch the ball to get the treats to

come out. Some ball launchers have adjustable settings, so you can make the game more challenging over time.

Dogs love to chew. It's a natural behavior that helps them keep their teeth clean and their jaws strong. But not all chew toys are created equal. Some are better than others, depending on your dog's needs and preferences.

There are a few different types of chew toys to choose from:

- <u>Rubber Toys</u> - These toys are durable and can withstand a lot of chewing. Some rubber toys are hollow, so you can fill them with treats or peanut butter to keep your dog engaged longer.
- <u>Rope Toys</u> - These toys are made from twisted or braided rope, which makes them great for chewing and playing tug-of-war. They're also good for your dog's dental health because the rope helps clean their teeth.
- <u>Edible Chew Toys</u> - These toys are made from natural materials, like rawhide or antlers, that your dog can chew on and consume. They're great for dogs who are aggressive chewers and need something to occupy their time and energy.

I hope your furry friend had a blast playing all those games while you run errands. But now that you're back, it's time to switch gears and focus on their nutritional needs. In the next part of this book, we'll delve into the wonderful world of nourishing your pup so it can continue to mentally and physically thrive. So put down that leash and pick up a fork because it's time to dig in!

Part 6

From Bowls to Bellies:
A Guide to Nourishing Your Pup

Do you ever wonder if your furry friend is getting the right nutrients they need to keep up with their endless energy? Are you tired of reading confusing labels on commercial dog food bags, wondering what exactly is in them? That no larger has to be your reality because, in this part, we will discuss the most important aspect of your dog's health - nutrition. From choosing the right type of food to understanding how much to feed them, we'll cover everything you need to know to ensure your pup has a happy and healthy tummy. Grab your forks (or should I say, your dog's bowls), and let's dig into this guide on nourishing your pup from bowls to bellies!

Nutrition

We will talk about a topic near and dear to every dog's heart: food! But it's not just about filling up that furry belly. As much as we all wish we could toss our furry friend a bag of chips and call it a day, the truth is that dogs, just like humans, need a balanced diet to stay healthy and strong. So, let's dive into the world of dog nutrition and find out what our four-legged friends need to chow down on.

To begin with, let's address the fundamentals. Dogs require a combination of nutrients from both animal and plant sources to flourish, which classifies them as omnivores. Animal-based proteins build strong muscles and bones, while plant-based nutrients such as vitamins, minerals, and fiber are essential for overall health and digestion. However, the exact ratio of meat to plant-based food depends on a few factors, such as age, size, and activity level. Typically, a diet that is abundant in protein and fat while containing moderate amounts of carbohydrates is what dogs need to maintain their health.

Now, let's talk about some specific nutrients that your dog needs. Protein is essential for muscle growth and repair and should comprise a significant portion of your dog's diet. Chicken, beef, lamb, fish, and eggs are excellent protein sources for dogs. You might know that not all protein sources are created equal, and some may be more easily digestible for your dog than others.

Next up, we have fat. Fat is an important energy source for dogs and helps with the absorption of certain vitamins. Fish oil, chicken fat, and vegetable oils are all considered beneficial fat sources for dogs. However, it's essential to remember that too much fat can lead to weight gain and other health problems, so feeding your dog a balanced diet is essential.

Carbohydrates in a dog's diet are crucial as they provide both energy and fiber to support their overall health. Whole grains, vegetables, and fruits are all excellent sources of carbohydrates for dogs. You might know that not all carbohydrates are created equal, and some may be more easily digestible for your dog than others.

In addition to these macronutrients, several micronutrients are essential for your dog's health. Essential vitamins and minerals, such as calcium, phosphorus, and vitamin D, are included in this group. It's important to ensure that your dog's diet includes a variety of foods to provide these essential nutrients.

Now that we've covered the basics of dog nutrition let's talk about some common misconceptions. One of the biggest misconceptions is that dogs need a grain-free diet. Although certain dogs may have allergies or sensitivities to particular grains, the majority of dogs are capable of digesting grains with ease. Some grains, such as brown rice and quinoa, can provide essential nutrients for your dog.

Another common misconception is that all commercial dog food is bad for your dog. While some lower-quality brands are out there, many commercial dog foods are carefully formulated to provide a balanced diet for your dog. It's essential to do your research and choose a high-quality brand that meets your dog's nutritional needs.

Finally, let's talk about treats. Treats can be a great way to reward your dog and provide some extra nutrients, but it's important to use them in moderation. Excessive treat consumption can result in weight gain and various health issues for dogs. When searching for treats for your dog, opt for those crafted using high-quality ingredients with minimal fat and calorie content.

Dog Feeding Chart

Feeding your furry friend can be tricky, especially if you're new to the dog-parent game. You want to ensure do give your pup all the nutrients they need, but you don't want to overfeed them and end up with a pudgy pooch.

That's where a dog feeding chart comes in handy. It can help you track how much to feed your dog based on his weight, activity level, and age.

Firstly, establish your dog's weight. You can do this by weighing him at home with a scale or taking him to the vet for a weigh-in. Once you know your dog's weight, you can use a feeding chart to determine how much to feed him.

Most dog food brands have a feeding chart on their packaging or website that provides recommendations on how much to feed your dog based on his weight. These recommendations are usually given in cups or grams.
It's important to note that the feeding chart is just a guideline. Every dog is different, and their individual needs may vary based on their activity level, age, and health condition.

For example, a senior dog may need fewer calories than a young, active pup. A dog with health issues may require a special diet or portion sizes recommended by a vet.
You must consider the type of food you're feeding your dog. Different brands and types of food may have different caloric densities and nutritional profiles.

If you are uncertain about the appropriate amount of food to give your dog, seek guidance from your veterinarian. Your veterinarian can offer customized suggestions based on your dog's requirements and make any necessary modifications to their diet.
In addition to following a feeding chart, monitoring your dog's weight and adjusting their portion sizes as needed is essential. If your dog is gaining weight, you may need to reduce their portion sizes or switch to lower-calorie food.

On the other hand, if your dog is losing weight or not maintaining a healthy weight, you may need to increase their portion sizes or switch to higher-calorie food.

Now that we've covered the basics of a dog's nutritional needs and the various types of food they can consume, you might wonder which is better: croquettes or home feeding? It's a conventional question. We'll dive into answering it next.

Croquettes Or Home feeding?

The great debate of croquettes versus home-cooked meals for dogs. It's a topic with dog owners scratching their heads and asking themselves, "What's the best option for my furry friend?" Well, fear not because we're going to break down the pros and cons of each option in a relatable, funny, and unique way.

Let's start with croquettes. Croquettes, or dry dog food, have been the go-to option for dog owners for decades. It's easy to store and serve and comes in various flavors and formulas for dogs with different needs. Plus, it's nutritionally balanced, so you will be sure your dog is getting all the nutrients they need.

However, some argue that croquettes aren't the healthiest option for dogs. Some brands use low-quality ingredients, such as fillers and by-products, that can harm dogs in the long run. Additionally, some dogs may have trouble digesting certain types of croquettes, leading to digestive issues and other health problems.

On the other hand, home-cooked meals for dogs can provide various benefits. For one, you have full control over your ingredients, so you can ensure your dog gets high-quality, nutritious food. If your dog has allergies or sensitivities to particular ingredients, preparing homemade meals can be an excellent alternative.

However, home-cooked meals can also be time-consuming and expensive. It's essential to ensure you're using the right balance of ingredients to meet your dog's nutritional needs, which can require some research and planning. Plus, if you're not careful, you can end up feeding your dog an unbalanced and potentially harmful diet.

So, which option is paramount for your dog? It ultimately depends on your lifestyle and your dog's needs. Croquettes may be the way to go if you have a busy schedule and need a convenient option. Just make sure you're choosing a superior brand that uses health-giving ingredients. On the other hand, having the time and resources to prepare home-cooked meals can be a great way to ensure your dog is getting the best possible nutrition.

Ultimately, the central thing is conferring with your veterinarian to determine your furry friend's best feeding plan. They can help you assess your dog's needs and make recommendations based on age, weight, breed, and activity level. With their guidance, you can decide whether croquettes or home-cooked meals are the best options for your furry friend.

While croquettes and home-cooked meals can be great options for your furry friend, it's important to remember that dogs should never consume certain foods. In the following chapter, we'll discuss some of the most common prohibited foods you should know to keep your dog healthy and safe.

Prohibited food

As dog owners, we all want to give our furry friends the best of everything, including food. However, we might not know that some human foods can be harmful and, in some cases, even deadly to our four-legged companions. Educating ourselves on what foods are prohibited for dogs to keep them safe and healthy is important.
Here's a list of prohibited foods for dogs.

Chocolate

Chocolate has theobromine and it is toxic to your furry friend. This is because dogs cannot metabolize theobromine as efficiently as humans, which can cause it to build up in their system to toxic levels.

Theobromine belongs to a class of chemicals called methylxanthines, which can cause many adverse effects in dogs, including increased heart rate, agitation, hyperactivity, seizures, and even death in severe cases. The brutality of the symptoms rests on the quantity of theobromine swallowed and the dog's size.

Theobromine is found in varying amounts in different types of chocolate, with darker chocolates and baked chocolate containing higher concentrations than milk chocolate. Even small amounts of chocolate can be toxic to dogs, especially in smaller breeds or those with preexisting medical conditions.

It's vital for dog owners to be aware of the potential dangers of theobromine and to keep chocolate and other foods containing this compound out of reach of their pets. A more comprehensive list of items that have this compound includes:

- Cocoa powder
- White chocolate (contains very little theobromine but can still be harmful in large amounts)
- Dark chocolate
- Milk chocolate
- Chocolate-covered espresso beans
- Chocolate-flavored desserts or drinks (for example, chocolate ice cream and hot chocolate)
- Baking chocolate
- Chocolate chips

- Chocolate cake or brownie mixes
- Chocolate-based spreads like Nutella
- Chocolate protein bars and other health bars containing chocolate
- Some medications and supplements containing cocoa or chocolate extract
- Some types of candy or energy bars that contain cocoa powder or chocolate.

Grapes and raisins

It turns out grapes and raisins can be pretty sneaky little dog snacks. While humans love to munch on them as a healthy snack or toss them into our trail mix, they can be pretty dangerous for our furry friends.

You see, grapes and raisins contain some mystery substance that hasn't yet been identified, and for dogs, it can cause serious health problems. Eating even a small amount of these fruity treats can lead to kidney failure, which you do not want your dog to experience. Grape or raisin poisoning symptoms include vomiting, diarrhea, lethargy, and dehydration.

Are you searching a good snack for your furry fiend? Stick to things like carrots, apples, or even some plain, unsalted popcorn (don't forget to share!).

Onions and garlic

Imagine that you are a food scientist studying the effects of different foods on the human body. You've extensively researched the health benefits and drawbacks of various fruits, vegetables, and spices. One day, you stumble upon a study that shows that onions and garlic can be toxic to dogs. You scratch your head and wonder why.

Well, it turns out that onions and garlic contain compounds called organosulfur compounds. These compounds can cause a type of anemia in dogs called Heinz body anemia. This condition occurs when the organosulfur compounds damage the red blood cells in your dog's body, causing them to rupture and die. As a result, your dog may experience symptoms like weakness, lethargy, pale gums, vomiting, and breathing difficulties.

Now, you may wonder why onions and garlic are toxic to dogs but not humans. The answer lies in the way that dogs metabolize these compounds. Humans have a much larger livers than dogs, which allows us to break down and process these compounds more effectively. On the other hand, dogs have a smaller livers, meaning these compounds can build up in their system and cause damage.

So, as a dog owner, keeping onions and garlic away from your furry friend is essential. That means no table scraps or leftover meals containing these ingredients.

Avocado

Despite being hailed as a superfood for humans, this delicious fruit can harm our furry friends. The culprit? The avocado plant contains a harmful substance called persin, which can be present in its leaves, bark, and fruit. It can instigate various symptoms in dogs, including retching, diarrhea, and difficulty breathing. It can sometimes lead to more severe complications like pancreatitis and heart failure. Yikes!

So, as tempting as it may be to share your avocado toast with your pup, it's best to resist the urge. Offer your dog treats that are safe for them to consume, such as carrots, apples, and peanut butter, and reserve avocados for human consumption.

Alcohol

Oh boy, where do I even start with this one? Let's just say that alcohol and dogs do not mix well. If your furry friend gets their paws on even a small amount of alcohol, it could be a recipe for disaster. Here's why... First of all, dogs are much smaller than humans, so even a small amount of alcohol can significantly impact their system. What might seem like a harmless sip to us could be toxic to our four-legged friends.

But it's not just the quantity of spirits that's the problem. It's also the fact that dogs metabolize alcohol differently than we do. While our bodies have enzymes that break down alcohol, dogs don't have as many of these enzymes. This means that liquor stays in their system for elongated periods and can cause more harm.

The effects of alcohol on dogs can range from mild to severe, depending on how much they've ingested. Some common symptoms include vomiting, diarrhea, loss of coordination, and even seizures or respiratory failure in extreme cases.

So, the bottom line is this: keep the alcohol away from your furry friend. It's not worth the risk, and plenty of other ways to have a good time with your pup don't involve booze.

Macadamia nuts

Macadamia nuts may look innocent and crunchy, but looks can be deceiving. You see, macadamia nuts contain a toxin that can cause some pretty gnarly symptoms in dogs. We're discussing things like vomiting, tremors, hyperthermia, and even temporary paralysis. Yeah, you read that right, paralysis! That's like when your legs stop working, and you're stuck on the couch binge-watching Netflix all day.

And let's not forget about the dreaded "macadamia nut butt." Yes, that's a real thing. These nuts can cause major tummy troubles and lead to messy accidents. I mean, we're talking about projectile pooping and explosive diarrhea here. Not a pretty sight.

Cooked bones

Do you know how some people love giving their pups a nice, juicy bone to chew on? Well, here's the deal - it's not always safe. When cooked, bones become more breakable and can easily fragment into shards. And those sharp pieces can wreak havoc on your pup's digestive system. The splinters can cause cuts and tears in your dog's mouth, throat, and intestines, and they can also lead to serious health issues like blockages and perforations.

Stick to safe, chewable toys for your furry friend and leave the bones for the humans to enjoy. Your pup will thank you for it!

Xylitol

Xylitol is a sneaky little devil that can wreak havoc on your furry friend! Xylitol is an artificial sweetener that can be frequently discovered in sugar-free gum, candy, and particular brands of peanut butter. While it may be harmless to humans, it's super toxic to dogs.

Here's the deal: when a dog ingests xylitol, it quickly gets absorbed into its bloodstream and causes its pancreas to release a surge of insulin. This can lead to a dangerous drop in blood sugar levels, known as hypoglycemia. In acute cases, indications of xylitol poisoning can include vomiting, loss of dexterity, convulsions, and even liver failure.

Caffeine

Caffeine is the ultimate wake-up call for humans but a nightmare for our furry friends! It turns out that dogs can't handle caffeine as well as we do. And I mean, can you blame them? We've all had that one cup of coffee that's made our heart race and hands shake. Well, imagine that feeling times ten for a little pup!

Just like chocolate, caffeine contains a chemical called methylxanthine, which acts as a stimulant to our central nervous system. When a dog ingests caffeine, it can cause many problems, such as vomiting, restlessness, heart palpitations, and muscle tremors. And let's face it. Those are some pretty unpleasant symptoms for any creature to deal with.

You might think, "But dogs aren't even supposed to drink coffee!" And you're right. But here's the thing – caffeine can be found in many other products, too. This list includes:

- Tea
- Energy drinks
- Soft drinks
- Some medications
- Ice cream
- Protein bars
- Some breakfast cereals

All of these contain caffeine in varying amounts. So, it's essential to keep an eye out for any foods or drinks that might have this pesky little chemical.

Fatty foods

Ah, fatty foods. They're delicious, right? Humans can indulge in a greasy burger or a big ol' plate of bacon without too much trouble. But for our furry friends, it's a different story. You see, dogs just can't handle the fat as we can.

When dogs eat fatty foods, it can inflict mayhem on their digestive systems. They might start vomiting or having diarrhea. And let's be real. Nobody wants to deal with that mess. Plus, all that fat can strain their pancreas, leading to pancreatitis. Pancreatitis can cause your dog to become extremely sick and even require hospitalization.

But why is fat so bad for dogs? In essence, it all boils down to their physical anatomy. Dogs have a different digestive system from ours and process fat differently. When they eat fatty foods, their bodies must work extra hard to break down all that fat. And if there's too much of it, their digestive system just can't keep up.

As a dog owner, keeping these prohibited foods away from your furry friend is essential. If you have any suspicion that your dog has consumed any of these food items, seek veterinary assistance immediately. Prevention is always better than cure, so provide your dog with a balanced and healthy diet, and avoid feeding them human foods.

Avoiding prohibited foods is crucial to keeping your pup safe, but sometimes even seemingly harmless foods can cause unexpected problems. In the next chapter, we'll explore the topic of food allergies and how they can impact your dog's health and well-being.

Food Allergies

As much as dogs love to eat anything and everything, sometimes certain foods don't agree with their stomachs. Like humans, dogs can also develop food allergies that may lead to various unpleasant symptoms. So, what are food allergies, and how can we identify them in our furry friends?

Imagine you're a dog and just ate a delicious bowl of kibble. But instead of feeling happy and satisfied, your tummy starts rumbling, and you break out in an itchy rash. That's what we humans call a food allergy!

It happens when the immune system of your furry fiend overreacts to an individual protein found in food. It's like your body is throwing a tantrum because it doesn't like what it just ate. When dogs ingest a protein, they are allergic to, their immune system responds by producing antibodies that trigger the release of histamine and other chemicals in the body.

Communal symptoms of food allergies in dogs include scratching, redness, swelling of the skin, and digestive issues like puking and diarrhea. The tricky thing about food allergies is that they can develop at anytime, even if a dog has been eating the same food for years without any problems. In dog food, you can easily find the following allergens: beef, chicken, dairy, eggs, corn, soy, and wheat.

If you suspect your dog is experiencing a food allergy, consult with your veterinarian to exclude any other potential underlying medical conditions. Your veterinarian may suggest an elimination diet to determine which foods your dog may be allergic to. This involves feeding your dog a diet that contains a single protein and carbohydrate source for several weeks until their symptoms subside. From there, you can gradually add other ingredients to see how your dog reacts.

So, what can you do to prevent food allergies in your dog? Regrettably, there is no entirely surefire approach to inhibit them. However, there are some steps you can take to reduce the likelihood of your dog developing allergies. First and foremost, avoid feeding your dog table scraps or other human foods that are high in fat, salt, or sugar. Choose high-grade commercial dog foods designed to fulfill your dog's dietetic requirements.

Before offering your dog homemade food, you must consult a veterinary to ensure that your furry friend gets all the required nutrients. It's also a good idea to rotate your dog's protein sources every few months to reduce the risk of developing allergies to a specific protein.

In conclusion, food allergies are a common problem that can cause many symptoms in dogs. Working with your veterinarian and preventing allergies can help keep your furry friend healthy and happy. And remember, just because your dog is allergic to certain foods doesn't mean they can't still enjoy a delicious meal – plenty of hypoallergenic dog foods and treats are sure to make your pup's taste buds happy.

Now that we've covered the importance of understanding dog food allergies, it's time to look at the practical side of feeding your furry friend. In the next chapter, we'll delve into the details of planning, preparing, and storing your dog's food to ensure they stay healthy and happy.

Planning, Preparation, And Storage of food

Meal prep is not just for gym-goers and busy professionals anymore. Dog owners can also benefit from a little bit of planning and preparation when it comes to their furry friend's meals. After all, your dog deserves the best, including tasty and nutritious meals prepared with love and care. This means knowing what types of food your dog can eat, how much they need, and when they'll eat it. It would be best to ask your veterinarian for the proper dog diet based on age, breed, and health issues.

Now that you have a plan, it's time to prepare some delicious meals for your furry friend. You can go about it in many ways, from making meals from scratch to using pre-made mixes or frozen meals. Whichever option you choose, ensure you're using top-notch ingredients and avoiding any foods that could make your pup sick.

Just like humans, dogs can enjoy various flavors and textures. If you're cooking from scratch, don't hesitate to get creative! You can whip up some delicious chicken and vegetable stir-fry or throw together a hearty beef and rice casserole. Just make sure to circumvent any elements that are toxic to dogs, like onions or garlic.

If you're using pre-made mixes, read the labels carefully. Some mixes might contain questionable ingredients, so you'll want to ensure you're choosing a high-quality option. And if you're going for frozen meals, check the ingredients list to ensure they're free from harmful additives or preservatives.

No matter what method you grasp, remember that your dog's health is the top priority. So go ahead and get cooking but use only the best ingredients and avoid anything that could upset your pup's stomach.

Here are the safe food-handling practices you must follow when preparing meals for your dog:
- Wash your hands
- Wash utensils and surfaces in contact with food,
- Cook food to the right temperature
- Store food correctly.

Let's talk about storage. It's important to have a system for storing your dog's food. This can include using airtight containers, portioning meals into individual servings, and labeling everything with the date and contents.

Other options are available if you are out all day or not having enough time to prepare meals for your dog. You can opt for pre-made meals or snacks or consider a meal delivery service specifically for dogs.

When feeding your dog, it's essential to establish and stick to a routine. This means providing your dog at the same time each day and avoiding sudden changes to its diet or feeding schedule.

By planning, preparing, and storing your dog's food properly, you can make sure they receive the best nutrition and care possible. Always remember that it is important to seek advice from your veterinarian before implementing significant alterations to your dog's feeding routine or diet. And most importantly, don't forget to give your dog plenty of love and snuggles – after all, that's the most essential ingredient in any meal.

Now that you've learned about the importance of proper planning, preparation, and storage of your dog's food, you may be ready to take things to the next level and start cooking some homemade meals for your furry friend. In the next part of this book, we'll explore some delicious and nutritious dog food recipes you can easily make in your kitchen.

Part 7
Fido's Feast:
Gourmet, Nutritious, and Delicious Recipes
for Your Canine Companion

Serving your pup the same old boring kibble every day will become a thing of the past when you learn to treat your furry friend to culinary delights fit for a king or queen... Delights you have prepared yourself. In this part of the book, I've got all the recipes you need to turn your dog's mealtimes into a gourmet feast. From healthy and nutritious meals to indulgent treats, you'll learn to prepare something for every palate and every occasion. Whether your dog is a picky eater or a voracious chowhound, tantalize their taste buds with these delicious and nutritious recipes. Bon appétit!

Basic Recipes

Sometimes, commercial dog food just doesn't cut it. It can contain unknown ingredients, artificial preservatives, and insufficient flavor to wag your dog's tail. Homemade dog food can help you! In this chapter, we'll explore the benefits of homemade dog food and provide five unique recipes to get your taste buds (and your furry friend's) dancing excitedly.

When you eat a meal, you want to know what's in it, right? You want to ensure you get all the nutrients you need and that the food is good for your body. The same goes for your furry friend. Cooking at home for your dog, you can control the ingredients and ensure he eats a delicious and nutritious meal. Plus, it can be a fun bonding activity between you and your pup!

Without further ado, let's get straight to the menu.

Chicken and Rice Bowl

Prep: 15 minutes | Cooking T.: 30 minutes | No.: 4 serv.

WHAT YOU NEED
- 1 lb. chicken breasts, chopped (boneless and skinless)
- 1 cup brown rice
- 1 cup carrots
- 1 cup chopped green beans
- 1/2 cup spinach
- 2 tbsp olive oil
- 2 cups water
- Salt and pepper to taste

STEPS
1. Heat olive oil in a pot on medium heat. Add the chicken and cook until seared on all borders.
2. Add rice, water, green beans, and chopped carrots to the pot. Stir well.
3. Bring to a boil, cover it, and lower the heat.
4. Allow the mixture to cook for about 25 minutes. The chicken becomes thoroughly cooked, and the rice tender.
5. Incorporate the spinach and flavor with salt and pepper.
6. Serve with love to your pup after it has been cooled.

Sweet Potato Beef Stew

Prep: 20 minutes | Cooking T.: 2 hours | No.: 6 serv.

WHAT YOU NEED
- 1 lb. beef stew meat, chopped
- 2 peeled sweet potatoes
- 2 cups chopped carrots
- 2 cups chopped green beans
- 2 tbsp olive oil
- 4 cups beef broth
- 2 tbsp tomato paste
- 1 tbsp dried thyme
- Salt and pepper to taste

STEPS
1. In a hefty pot, heat olive oil over standard heat. Put in the beef and cook until scorched on all sides.
2. Add sweet potatoes, carrots, green beans, beef broth, tomato paste, and thyme to the pot. Stir well.
3. Bring to a boil, then lessen heat to low and place the lid on the pot.
4. Simmer for about 2 hours. Beef becomes soft, and vegetables become tender.
5. Season with salt and pepper to taste.
6. Cool and serve your dog.

Salmon and Quinoa Mix

Prep: 10 minutes | Cooking T.: 20 minutes | No.: 4 serv.

WHAT YOU NEED
- 1 lb. fresh salmon, chopped
- 1 cup quinoa
- 1 cup sweet peppers, chopped
- 1/2 cup zucchini, chopped
- 1/2 cup cherry tomatoes, chopped
- 2 tbsp olive oil

- 2 cups water
- Salt and pepper to taste

STEPS

1. In a big pan, heat olive oil over moderate heat. Add the salmon and cook until seared on all sides.
2. Add quinoa, water, sweet peppers, zucchini, and cherry tomatoes to the pot. Stir well.
3. Bring to a boil, then decrease the heat to low and place the lid on the pan.
4. Cook for about 18-20 minutes. Quinoa becomes tender, and the salmon become cooked through.
5. Season with pepper and salt.
6. Cool and dish out.

Vegetarian Lentil Stew

Prep: 10 minutes | Cooking T.: 40 minutes | No.: 4 serv.

WHAT YOU NEED

- 1 cup green lentils, drained
- 2 tbsp olive oil
- 1 onion, chopped
- 2 cloves garlic, minced
- 2 carrots, chopped
- 2 celery stalks, chopped
- 1 tsp dried thyme
- 1 tsp paprika
- 4 cups vegetable broth
- Salt and pepper, to taste

STEPS

1. Heat the olive oil over moderate heat in a sizeable pot or Dutch oven. Add the onion and garlic, and sauté until softened. This will take roughly 5 minutes.
2. Add the carrots and celery and cook for an added 5 minutes. Now they begin to soften.
3. Add the thyme and paprika and stir to coat the vegetables.
4. Add the lentils to the pot.
5. Bring to a boil with vegetable broth.

6. Cut the heat and let cook for about 30 minutes. The lentils become tender.
7. Add salt and pepper to taste.

Turkey and Vegetable Medley

Prep: 15 minutes | Cooking T.: 25 minutes | No.: 4 serv.

WHAT YOU NEED
- 1 lb. ground turkey
- 1 tbsp olive oil
- 1 onion, chopped
- cloves garlic, minced
- 2 carrots, peeled and diced
- 2 stalks of celery, diced
- 1 sweet potato, peeled
- 1/2 cup frozen peas
- 1/2 cup frozen green beans
- 2 cups low-sodium chicken broth

STEPS
1. In a sizeable pot, heat the olive oil over moderate heat. Put in the garlic and onion. Cook for about 5 minutes.
2. Add the ground turkey and cook for about 8 minutes, stirring every 2 minutes.
3. Add the celery, carrots, sweet potato, frozen green beans, frozen peas, and chicken broth.
4. Bring to a boil and let simmer for 18 minutes with reduced heat until vegetables are tender.
5. Serve cooled.

With these easy recipes, you'll give your dog only the healthy and nutritious meals that he will love. We're going to up the healthy ante in the next chapter.

Healthy Recipes

Healthy meals can help preclude diabetes, obesity, and heart problems in your furry friend. In this chapter, we'll cover five unique recipes packed with all the necessary nutrients and vitamins your furry friend needs to stay healthy and happy. You will surely be a hit with these easy recipes with your dog. So, let's get cooking!

Chicken and Kale Delight

Prep: 15 Minutes | Cooking T.: 30 Minutes | No.: 6 Serv.

WHAT YOU NEED
- 1 lb. boneless, skinless chicken breast, cut into small pieces
- 1 cup chopped kale
- 1 sweet potato, peeled and cubed
- 1 cup rice
- 1 tbsp coconut oil
- 1 tsp dried basil
- 2 cups water

STEPS
1. In a big pot, heat coconut oil over moderate heat. Add the chicken and char lightly.
2. Add sweet potato and kale to the pot and sauté for about 4 minutes until slightly tender.
3. Add brown rice, basil, and water and stir.
4. Bring to a boil, lessen heat, and simmer for 25 to 30 minutes. So, the rice is wholly cooked.
5. Let cool, then serve to your pup.

Beef and Carrot Casserole

Prep: 20 Minutes | Cooking T.: 1 Hour | No.: 8 Serv.

WHAT YOU NEED
- 1 lb. ground beef
- 2 cups chopped carrots
- 1 cup frozen peas

- 1 cup quinoa
- 1 tbsp olive oil
- 1 tsp dried thyme
- 3 cups water

STEPS

1. Preheat your oven to 375°F.
2. In a big frypan, heat olive oil over moderate heat. Put in the ground beef and cook until browned.
3. Add carrots and peas to the pan and cook for 5 to 7 minutes until they become tender.
4. Add quinoa, thyme, and water to the skillet and stir.
5. Bring to a boil, lower the heat, and cook for 15 minutes.
6. Relocate the blend to a baking pan and cook for about 35 minutes. Now it will be golden and brown.
7. Let it cool, then serve to your furry friend.

Salmon and Spinach Surprise

Prep: 10 Minutes | Cooking T.: 20 Minutes | No.: 4 Serv.

WHAT YOU NEED

- 1 lb. salmon fillet, cut into small pieces
- 2 cups chopped spinach
- 1 cup cooked quinoa
- 1 tbsp coconut oil
- 1 tsp dried dill
- 2 cups water

STEPS

1. In a sizeable pot, heat coconut oil over moderate heat. Add salmon and cook; it becomes moderately browned.
2. Add spinach to the pot and sauté for about 3 minutes until a little wilted.
3. Add cooked quinoa, water, and dill to the pot and stir.
4. Bring to a boil, lessen the heat, and cook for 12-12 minutes. The salmon is thoroughly cooked.
5. Let cool, then serve to your pup.

Turkey and Vegetable Stew

Prep: 20 minutes | Cooking T.: 45 minutes | No.: 6-8 serv.

WHAT YOU NEED
- 1 lb. ground turkey
- 1 cup quinoa, rinsed
- 2 cups chicken broth
- 1 sweet potato
- 1 zucchini, chopped
- 1 carrot, chopped
- 1 cup spinach, chopped
- 1 tbsp olive oil

STEPS
1. In a hefty pot, heat the olive oil over moderate heat. Put in the ground turkey and cook for about 7 minutes.
2. Add the quinoa, chicken broth, sweet potato (peeled and chopped), zucchini, and carrot to the pot. Mix well.
3. Bring the blend to a boil, lessen the heat, and put the lid over the pot.
4. Simmer for 30 minutes; now, quinoa and vegetables are tender.
5. Incorporate the spinach and wilt for about 3 minutes.
6. Allow the stew to cool and offer it to your pup.

Salmon and Sweet Potato Mash

Prep: 10 minutes | Cooking T.: 20 minutes | No.: 4 serv.

WHAT YOU NEED
- 2 cups cooked salmon, flaked
- 2 cups sweet potato
- 1 cup peas, cooked
- 1 tbsp coconut oil
- 1 tsp dried parsley

STEPS

1. Combine the salmon, sweet potato (cooked and mashed), peas, coconut oil, and parsley in a large bowl.
2. Mash the ingredients together until well combined.
3. Serve the mash to your pup while it's still warm.

We've covered the territory of food that is generally healthy for you to prepare for your pup, but let's now move on to recipes for dog disorders.

Disorder Recipes

Just like humans, dogs can suffer from various health disorders that affect their quality of life. While some conditions require veterinary treatment, others can be managed or even alleviated through diet. In this chapter, we'll explore recipes for dog disorders designed to provide the specific nutrients and compounds to support your furry friend's health and well-being.

I've got you covered, from recipes for dogs with digestive issues to those with joint problems. Our recipes use wholesome, nutrient-dense ingredients that are easy to ingredients that are packed with beneficial nutrients and easy to digest. Whether your dog is dealing with a chronic condition, or you want to support their health and well-being, these recipes are a great place to start. So, let's get cooking!

Chicken and Carrot Stew

Prep: 10 minutes | Cooking T.: 35 minutes | No.: 4 serv.

WHAT YOU NEED

- 1 lb. boneless, skinless chicken breasts
- 2 cups chopped carrots
- 2 cups chicken broth
- 1 cup white rice
- 2 tbsp olive oil

STEPS

1. In a medium pot, heat the olive oil over medium heat.
2. Put in the chicken (cut into bite-sized pieces) and cook until browned all over.
3. Add the chopped carrots and chicken to the pot and boil. Cook for 20 minutes on low heat.
4. Add the rice to the pot, stir well, cover, and cook for a further 15 minutes. The rice will be tender, and the stew thickened.
5. Cool and serve.

Beef and Rice Porridge

Prep: 10 minutes | Cooking T.: 40 minutes | No.: 4 serv.

WHAT YOU NEED
- 1 lb. ground beef
- 2 cups white rice
- 4 cups beef broth
- 1 cup diced carrots
- 1/2 cup frozen green beans

STEPS
1. In a big crock or Dutch oven, brown the ground beef atop moderate heat.
2. Add the white rice, beef broth, and diced carrots to the pot, boil, then lower the heat to a minimum and cook for 30 minutes.
3. Add the frozen green beans to the pot and cook for a further 10 minutes. The porridge is thickened, and the rice is fully cooked.
4. Cool and serve.

Turkey and Green Beans

Prep: 10 minutes | Cooking T.: 20 minutes | No.: 4 serv.

WHAT YOU NEED
- 1 lb. ground turkey
- 1 can of green beans
- 1 cup cooked brown rice
- 1 tbsp olive oil
- 1/4 cup chopped parsley

STEPS
1. Heat olive oil in a medium frypan over high heat.
2. Put in the ground turkey and brow for about 7 minutes.
3. Add the green beans and brown rice and stir well.
4. Cook for a further 5 minutes. Now everything is heated through.

5. Stir in chopped parsley after removing from heat.
6. Allow to cool before serving.

Fish and Sweet Potato Stew

Prep: 15 minutes | Cooking T.: 30 minutes | No.: 6 serv.

WHAT YOU NEED
- 1 lb. white fish fillets
- 2 sweet potatoes, peeled and diced
- 1 can of tomatoes
- 1 onion
- 2 cloves garlic
- 1 tsp ground cumin
- 1 tsp smoked paprika
- 4 cups low-sodium chicken broth
- 1 tbsp olive oil

STEPS
1. Heat olive oil in a sizeable pot over moderate heat.
2. Put in the minced garlic and the chopped onion and cook until softened – for about 5 minutes.
3. Mix well with the diced tomatoes, sweet potatoes, smoked paprika, and cumin.
4. Add in the chicken broth and allow to come to a boil.
5. Decrease heat and cook for about 20 minutes until sweet potatoes are tender.
6. Add the fillets and cook for an added 5 to 7 minutes. That is until the fish is cooked all the way through.
7. Remove from heat and let cool.

Carrot and Turkey Stew

Prep: 10 Minutes | Cooking T.: 30 Minutes | No.: 4 Serv.

WHAT YOU NEED
- 1 lb. ground turkey

- 2 cups carrots
- 1 cup green beans
- 1 cup spinach
- 2 tbsp olive oil
- 1 tbsp parsley
- 1 tbsp rosemary
- 1 cup low-sodium chicken broth

STEPS

1. In a medium frying pan, heat olive oil over moderate heat.
2. Add ground turkey and cook until browned - 8 to 10 minutes.
3. Add green beans and chopped carrots and cook for a further 5 minutes.
4. Add chopped spinach and cook an added 5 to 7 minutes until wilted.
5. Add dried parsley, dried rosemary, and low-sodium chicken broth.
6. Cut heat to low, put the lid on, and cook an added 10 to 15 minutes. Now the vegetables are very soft.
7. Take away from heat and let cool before serving.

I hope you enjoyed those tasty and healthy recipes for pups with special dietary needs. But now, let's talk about something that affects many dogs, especially those who love to chow down: the struggle to maintain a healthy weight. Like humans, our furry friends must watch their waistlines and avoid excessive treats and fatty foods. Don't worry, though. They can still enjoy delicious meals and treats with the help of some low-fat recipes. So, let's walk over to the next chapter and get cooking!

Low-fat Recipes

We all desire our furry friends to be healthy and full of bliss. For dogs who need to lose weight or have health conditions requiring a low-fat diet, it can be challenging to find nutritious and low-fat food. In this chapter, I will provide you with five unique and tasty low-fat dog food recipes that will keep your pup satisfied and healthy. These recipes are simple and will give your dog all the required nutrients.

Turkey and Brown Rice Medley

Prep: 10 minutes | Cooking T.: 45 minutes | No.: 6-8 serv.

WHAT YOU NEED
- 1 lb. ground turkey
- 2 cups brown rice, cooked
- 1 cup carrots
- 1 cup green beans
- 1 cup peas
- 1 tbsp olive oil

STEPS
1. Preheat your oven to 375°F.
2. In a frying pan, heat olive oil over moderate heat.
3. Add ground turkey and cook until browned.
4. Put in the chopped green beans and the chopped carrots and sauté for 5 minutes.
5. Add peas and cooked brown rice to the pan and mix well.
6. Transfer all the ingredients to a baking dish and cook for 20 minutes.
7. Pull out from the oven, cool, and serve.

Chicken and Sweet Potato Mash

Prep: 10 minutes | Cooking T.: 30 minutes | No.: 6-8 serv.

WHAT YOU NEED
- 2 boneless chicken breasts, cubed
- 2 cups sweet potato, cubed
- 1 cup green beans
- 1 tbsp olive oil

STEPS
1. Preheat your oven to 375°F. moderate
2. Heat olive oil over medium heat in a pan.
3. Add cubed chicken breasts and brow them.
4. Add cubed sweet potatoes and chopped green beans to the pan and cook for about 4 minutes.
5. Transfer all the ingredients to a baking dish and cook for 20 minutes.
6. Remove from the oven, cool, and serve.

Beef and Barley Stew

Prep: 10 minutes | Cooking T.: 60 minutes | No.: 6-8 serv.

WHAT YOU NEED
- 1 lb. beef stew meat, cubed
- 2 cups barley, cooked
- 1 cup carrots
- 1 cup green beans
- 2 tbsp olive oil

STEPS
1. In a Dutch oven, heat olive oil atop moderate heat.
2. Add cubed beef stew meat and cook until browned.
3. Add the chopped green beans and the chopped carrots and panfry for about 6 minutes.
4. Add cooked barley and 4 cups of water to the Dutch oven.
5. Bring to a boil and simmer for 40 minutes with reduced heat.
6. Remove from heat, cool, and serve.

Salmon and Sweet Potato Patties

Prep: 10 minutes | Cooking T.: 20 minutes | No.: 6-8 patties

WHAT YOU NEED

- 1 can of salmon, drained and flaked
- 2 cups sweet potato, boiled and mashed
- 1 egg
- 1 tbsp parsley
- 1 tbsp olive oil

STEPS

1. Preheat your oven to 375°F.
2. Combine flaked salmon, mashed sweet potato, egg, and chopped parsley in a medium bowl.
3. Mix until you obtain a dough-like consistency.
4. Shape the mixture into 6 to 8 patties.
5. Heat olive oil in a skillet over moderate heat.
6. Add the patties to the frying pan and cook on both sides for 2 to 3 minutes.
7. Transfer the patties to a dish and cook for 10 minutes.
8. Remove from the oven. Cool, and let your doggo enjoy!

Vegetarian Chickpea Stew

Prep: 10 minutes | Cooking T.: 30 minutes | No.: 4-6 serv.

WHAT YOU NEED

- 1 can chickpeas
- 1/2 cup brown rice
- 1/2 cup diced sweet potatoes
- 1/2 cup green beans, trimmed and chopped
- 1/4 cup diced onion
- 2 cups vegetable broth
- 1 tbsp olive oil

STEPS

1. Cook the brown rice concurring to package directions, in the low-sodium vegetable broth.

2. In a pan, pan the diced onion in olive oil until it becomes translucent.
3. Put the sweet potatoes and green beans in and cook for 5 minutes.
4. Add the chickpeas (drained and rinsed) and vegetables to the pot and allow to produce a boil.
5. Lower the heat to a minimum and cook for about 18 minutes.
6. Add cooked brown rice to the and cook for an added 5 to 7 minutes.
7. Serve once it has cooled.

If your furry friend needs to shed a few pounds, the low-fat recipes in this chapter have you covered. But now it's time to kick things up a notch in the next chapter with some weight regulation recipes. These meals will help your pup feel appeased, minus the extra calories.

Weight Regulation Recipes

Maintaining a healthy weight is essential for your furry friend's overall well-being. Overweightness can lead to various health issues, including joint problems, heart disease, and diabetes. Well-balanced diets and controlled portions are essential for feeding your dog correctly. So he will maintain the right weight. In this chapter, we will discuss recipes specifically designed for weight regulation. These recipes are low in calories and fat while providing your dog with all the necessary nutrients to stay healthy and happy. So, let's get started on the path to a healthier, happier pup!

Lean Turkey and Sweet Potato Mash

Prep: 15 Minutes | Cooking T.: 30 Minutes | No.: 4 Serv.

WHAT YOU NEED
- 1 lb. ground turkey
- 1/4 tsp dried thyme
- 1 cup cooked sweet potato, mashed
- 1 tbsp olive oil
- 1/2 tsp dried rosemary
- 1 cup cooked green beans
- 1 tsp dried parsley
- 1/4 tsp ground black pepper

STEPS
1. In a large frypan, heat olive oil over moderate heat.
2. Add ground turkey and cook until browned and cooked through.
3. Add green beans and mashed sweet potato to the skillet and mix well.
4. Add dried parsley, thyme, rosemary, and ground black pepper to the frypan and mix well.
5. Serve to your dog once it has cooled to room temperature.

Carrot and Lentil Stew

Prep: 10 Minutes | Cooking T.: 45 Minutes | No.: 4 Serv.

WHAT YOU NEED

- 1 cup dry lentils
- 4 cups low-sodium chicken broth
- 1 cup chopped carrots
- 1 cup celery, chopped
- 1/4 cup parsley, chopped
- 1 tbsp olive oil

STEPS

1. In a medium saucepan, let the chicken broth come to a boil.
2. Add lentils, chopped carrots, and chopped celery to the pot.
3. Lower the heat to a minimum and cook for about 40 minutes or until the lentils and vegetables are soft.
4. Add olive oil and chopped parsley to the pot and mix well.
5. Serve to your dog once it has cooled to room temperature.

Turkey and Vegetable Stir-Fry

Prep: 10 Minutes | Cooking T.: 15 Minutes | No.: 4 Serv.

WHAT YOU NEED

- 1 lb. ground turkey
- 2 cups mixed vegetables (broccoli, carrots, green beans)
- 1 tbsp olive oil
- 1/4 cup chicken broth
- 1 tbsp soy sauce
- 1 tsp minced garlic
- 1 tsp minced ginger

STEPS

1. Heat olive oil atop moderate to high heat in a medium skillet frying pan.
2. Add ground turkey and cook until the turkey is well-browned and adequately cooked.
3. Mix well with mixed vegetables, ginger, and garlic in the frying pan.
4. Add low-sodium chicken broth and low-sodium soy sauce to the frying pan and mix well.
5. Lower the heat to a minimum and cook for about 8 minutes. So, you could pierce the vegetables with a knife.
6. Serve to your dog once it has cooled to room temperature.

Delicious Broccoli Chicken

Prep: 15 minutes | Cooking T.: 25 minutes | No.: 4 serv.

WHAT YOU NEED
- 1 lb. boneless, skinless chicken breasts
- 2 cups broccoli florets
- 1 red bell pepper
- 1 yellow onion
- 1 tbsp olive oil
- 1 tbsp cornstarch
- 1 tbsp soy sauce
- 1 tsp honey
- 1/2 tsp garlic powder
- Salt and pepper to taste

STEPS
1. In a medium frying pan, heat the olive oil atop moderate heat.
2. Put in the chicken (thinly sliced) and cook until browned so that the insides are no longer pink – about 6 minutes.
3. Add the sliced bell pepper, broccoli, and onion to the skillet and continue cooking for another 5 to 7 minutes. The vegetables will be tender.
4. Mix the cornstarch, honey, garlic powder, soy sauce, salt, and pepper in a medium bowl.
5. Add the sauce on the chicken and vegetables in the pan and mix until everything is evenly coated.
6. Cook for a further 5 minutes to thicken the sauce.
7. Cool and serve your dog!

Turkey and Sweet Potato Chili

Prep: 20 minutes | Cooking T.: 1 hour 30 minutes | No.: 6 serv.

WHAT YOU NEED
- 1 lb. ground turkey

- 3 cloves garlic
- 1 onion
- 2 sweet potatoes, peeled and cubed
- 1 green bell pepper
- 1 red bell pepper
- 1 can (14.5 ounces) tomatoes
- 1 can (15 ounces) black beans
- 1 tbsp chili powder
- 1/2 tsp paprika
- 1 tsp cumin
- Salt and pepper to taste

STEPS

1. In a medium pot, cook the ground turkey over high heat until browned and cooked.
2. Include the minced garlic and the diced onion in the pot and cook for another 2 to 3 minutes. The onion will be see-through.
3. Next, add the sweet potatoes, diced bell peppers, tomatoes, black beans (drained and rinsed), chili powder, paprika, cumin, salt, and pepper.
4. Stir everything together until evenly combined.
5. Bring the chili to a simmer and lessen the heat to low.
6. Put the lid over the pot and allow the chili to simmer for 1 hour, stirring occasionally.
7. After 1 hour, remove the lid from the pot and let the chili cook for an extra 18 minutes to thicken.
8. Serve to the pup, so he can enjoy it!

I've provided recipes perfect for dogs needing help keeping slim and trimming. But now it's time to reward your pup for all their hard work with some tasty treats in the next chapter!

Treat Recipes

We all know how much our furry friends love treats. It seems as though dogs have a vague sense dedicated to detecting them. And let's face it, seeing those wagging tails and happy faces when we bring out a bag of treats is the best feeling ever.

But, as much as we love spoiling our pups, we also want to ensure that what we give them is healthy and nutritious. That's why I've compiled this chapter full of tasty and wholesome treat recipes that your dog will love. And the best part is that these treats are delicious and good for your dog's health. So, whether you want to reward them for being a good boy or girl or simply want to share a special moment with them, you can feel good about what you're giving them.

Pull up your sleeves because we're about to get baking!

Peanut Butter and Banana Bites

Prep: 10 minutes | Cooking T.: 0 minutes | No.: 15-20 treats

WHAT YOU NEED
- 1 ripe banana
- 1/2 cup natural peanut butter
- 1 1/2 cups rolled oats
- 1/4 cup honey
- 1/4 cup ground flaxseed

STEPS
1. Mix the mashed banana, peanut butter, and honey in a medium-sized bowl.
2. Mix well with the rolled oats and ground flaxseed.
3. Transfer this mixture into small balls on a lined baking sheet.
4. Refrigerate for 30 to 50 minutes until the bites are firm.

Sweet Potato Chews

Prep: 10 minutes | Cooking T.: 2 hours | No.: Varies depending on sweet potato size

WHAT YOU NEED
- 1 large sweet potato
- 1 tbsp olive oil

STEPS
1. Preheat your oven to 225°F and arrange parchment paper on a baking sheet.
2. Cut the potato into slim slices, about 1/4 inch thick.
3. In a medium bowl, blend the potato slices with some olive oil until glazed.
4. Place the slices in one layer on the baking sheet.
5. Cook for 2 hours. Now the slices will be dry and chewy.
6. Allow the slices to cool before serving.

Carrot and Apple Treats

Prep: 15 minutes | Cooking T.: 25 minutes | No.: 20-25 treats

WHAT YOU NEED
- 1 cup grated carrot
- 1 cup grated apple
- 2 eggs
- 1/4 cup coconut flour
- 1/4 cup rolled oats
- 1/4 cup almond flour
- 1/4 cup fresh parsley

STEPS
1. Preheat your oven to 350°F.
2. Combine the grated carrot, grated apple, and eggs in a big bowl.
3. Add the coconut flour, rolled oats, almond flour, and chopped parsley and mix well.
4. Transfer each mixture's spoonful onto the baking sheet covered with parchment paper. Then, crush with a fork.
5. Bake for about 25 minutes: the treats become golden brown.
6. Let the treats cool before serving.

Salmon Jerky

Prep: 10 minutes | Cooking T.: 4 hours | No.: Varies depending on salmon fillet size

WHAT YOU NEED
- 1 lb. salmon fillet, skin removed
- 2 tbsp honey
- 2 tbsp soy sauce
- 2 tbsp water
- 1 tsp garlic powder

STEPS
1. Preheat your oven to 200°F.
2. Cut the salmon fillet into thin strips, about 1/4 inch thick.
3. Combine the honey, water, garlic powder, and soy sauce in a medium bowl.
4. Dip each salmon strip into this mixture until the salmon is well coated.
5. Place the strips in one layer on the baking sheet covered with parchment paper.
6. Bake for 4 hours or until the strips are dry and chewy.
7. Let the strips cool before serving.

Sweet Potato and Peanut Butter Bites for Pups

Prep: 10 Minutes | Cooking T.: 25 Minutes | No.: 24 Treats

WHAT YOU NEED
- 1 cup whole wheat flour
- 1/2 cup applesauce, unsweetened
- 1/4 cup natural peanut butter
- 1/4 cup water
- 1/2 tsp baking powder

STEPS
1. Preheat your oven to 350°F.
2. In a medium bowl, mix well all the ingredients to form a thick dough.
3. Roll out the dough on a dusted plane until it is 1/4 inch thick.
4. Create shapes from the dough with a cookie cutter.

5. Place them onto a baking sheet covered with parchment paper.
6. Cook for 20-25 minutes: the treats will be brown and crispy.
7. Take out from the oven and allow the treats to cool down totally.
8. Serve to the pup so he can enjoy it!

We've concluded this section of the book. Congrats! You're nearly there to become a certified dog cook.

Conclusion

We've come to the end of our journey with the THE COMPLETE DOG BIBLE. Hopefully, by now, you're feeling like a bona fide dog whisperer, and your furry friend is now the obedient, well-behaved companion you always knew they could be.

Training a dog isn't always easy. It takes patience, dedication, and a lot of hard work. But trust me. It's all worth it at the end when you have a happy, healthy, and well-trained dog by your side.

And with the THE COMPLETE DOG BIBLE, achieving that goal has made it easier than ever. From potty training to nutrition, right down to physical exercises to mental stimulation, we've covered all the bases to help you and your pup live your best lives together.

But don't rely on my word - just ask your furry friend! I'm willing to bet that they're happier and healthier than ever, thanks to the training and care you've provided them.

And speaking of care, let's not forget about the cookbook section of this book. We all know how much dogs love their treats, and now you can rest assured that your pup is getting the best possible nutrition with delicious and nutritious recipes coming straight from your kitchen.

Whether you're a pup parent novice or a master trainer, THE COMPLETE DOG BIBLE is your one-stop-shop for all things canine. I positively hope that the woof-worthy advice and tail-wagging tricks you've picked up along the way will help you and your furry sidekick create an unbreakable bond. Keep those tails twitching, and the treats ever available! Remember, with a little patience, practice, and plenty of treats, you and your furry friend can conquer any obstacle together.

I send you and your pup all the best wishes. May your days be filled with tail wags, wet noses, and endless amounts of love and joy.

Share the love with another canine lover and their pooch by sharing this book or leaving a review!

References

1. *Puppy parties and beyond: The role of early age socialization practices on adult dog behavior.* (n.d.). PubMed Central (PMC). https://www.ncbi.nlm.nih.gov/pmc/articles/PMC6067676/

2. *Massage therapy for dogs and cats.* (n.d.). PubMed. https://pubmed.ncbi.nlm.nih.gov/25454377/

3. *The role of oxytocin in the dog—owner relationship.* (n.d.). PubMed Central (PMC). https://www.ncbi.nlm.nih.gov/pmc/articles/PMC6826447/

4. *Integrative model of human-animal interactions: A one health—one welfare systemic approach to studying HAI.* (n.d.). Frontiers. https://www.frontiersin.org/articles/10.3389/fvets.2022.656833/full

5. *The implicit reward value of the owner's face for dogs.* (20, August). PubMed Central (PMC). https://www.ncbi.nlm.nih.gov/pmc/articles/PMC8355952/

6. *Incentive motivation in pet dogs — preference for constant vs varied food rewards.* (n.d.). PubMed Central (PMC). https://www.ncbi.nlm.nih.gov/pmc/articles/PMC6021384/

7. *Cognitive aging in dogs.* (n.d.). PubMed Central (PMC). https://www.ncbi.nlm.nih.gov/pmc/articles/PMC5841136/

8. *Encouraging dog walking for health promotion and disease prevention.* (2018, May). PubMed Central (PMC). https://www.ncbi.nlm.nih.gov/pmc/articles/PMC6124971/

9. *Healthy, active aging for people and dogs.* (n.d.). PubMed Central (PMC). https://www.ncbi.nlm.nih.gov/pmc/articles/PMC8215343/

10. *How powerful is a dog's nose?* (n.d.). Phoenix Veterinary Center - Small Animal Hospital in Phoenix, AZ Phoenix Veterinary Center - Veterinarian in Phoenix, AZ US. https://phoenixvetcenter.com/blog/214731-how-powerful-is-a-dogs-nose